DATE DUE

APR – 5 2000	
JUL 1 0 2000	OCT 2 9 2005
NOV – 6 2000	OCT 1 0 2007
DEC 2 9 2001	
NOV 3 0 2002	
DEC 0 6 2002 NOV 2 3 2003 DEC 3 0 2003	
OCT 1 6 2004 NOV – 6 2004	
NOV 2 7 2004	
AUG 2 2 2005	

RENEWALS
362-0438

The Library Store   #47-0106

Leaders of Ancient Greece

Other Books in the History Makers Series:

Leaders of Ancient Greece

By Don Nardo

Lucent Books
P.O. Box 289011, San Diego, CA 92198-9011

Library of Congress Cataloging-in-Publication Data

Nardo, Don, 1947–
    Leaders of ancient Greece / by Don Nardo.
        p.   cm. — (History makers)
    Includes bibliographical references and index.
    Summary: Discusses the contributions of eight influential leaders
of ancient Greece, including Solon, Themistocles, Pericles, Alcibiades,
Epaminondas, Philip, Alexander, and Pyrrhus.
    ISBN 1-56006-543-5 (lib. bdg. : alk. paper)
    1. Greece—Kings and rulers—Biography—Juvenile literature.
2. Kings and rulers, Ancient—Biography—Juvenile literature.
3. Greece—Politics and government—To 146 B.C.—Juvenile literature.
[1. Greece—Kings and rulers.   2. Greece—Politics and government—To
146 B.C.   3. Kings, queens, rulers, etc.]   I. Title.   II. Series.
DF208.N37   1999
938'.009'9—dc21   99-18176
[B]   CIP
                                                                              AC

Copyright 1999 by Lucent Books, Inc.
P.O. Box 289011, San Diego, California 92198-9011

Printed in the U.S.A.

CONTENTS

The literary form most often referred to as "multiple biography" was perfected in the first century A.D. by Plutarch, a perceptive and talented moralist and historian who hailed from the small town of Chaeronea in central Greece. His most famous work, *Parallel Lives*, consists of a long series of biographies of noteworthy ancient Greek and Roman statesmen and military leaders. Frequently, Plutarch compares a famous Greek to a famous Roman, pointing out similarities in personality and achievements. These expertly constructed and very readable tracts provided later historians and others, including playwrights like Shakespeare, with priceless information about prominent ancient personages and also inspired new generations of writers to tackle the multiple biography genre.

The Lucent History Makers series proudly carries on the venerable tradition handed down from Plutarch. Each volume in the series consists of a set of six to eight biographies of important and influential historical figures who were linked together by a common factor. In *Rulers of Ancient Rome*, for example, all the figures were generals, consuls, or emperors of either the Roman Republic or Empire; while the subjects of *Fighters Against American Slavery*, though they lived in different places and times, all shared the same goal, namely the eradication of human servitude. Mindful that politicians and military leaders are not (and never have been) the only people who shape the course of history, the editors of the series have also included representatives from a wide range of endeavors, including scientists, artists, writers, philosophers, religious leaders, and sports figures.

Each book is intended to give a range of figures—some well known, others less known; some who made a great impact on history, others who made only a small impact. For instance, by making Columbus's initial voyage possible, Spain's Queen Isabella I, featured in *Women Leaders of Nations*, helped to open up the New World to exploration and exploitation by the European powers. Unarguably, therefore, she made a major contribution to a series of events that had momentous consequences for the entire world. By contrast, Catherine II, the eighteenth-century Russian queen, and Golda Meir, the modern Israeli prime minister, did not play roles of global impact; however, their policies and actions significantly influenced the historical development of both their own countries and their regional neighbors. Regardless of their relative importance in the greater historical scheme, all of the figures chronicled in the History Makers series made contributions to posterity; and their public achievements, as well as what is known about their private lives, are presented and evaluated in light of the most recent scholarship.

In addition, each volume in the series is documented and substantiated by a wide array of primary and secondary source quotations. The primary source quotes enliven the text by presenting eyewitness views of the times and culture in which each history maker lived; while the secondary source quotes, taken from the works of respected modern scholars, offer expert elaboration and/ or critical commentary. Each quote is footnoted, demonstrating to the reader exactly where biographers find their information. The footnotes also provide the reader with the means of conducting additional research. Finally, to further guide and illuminate readers, each volume in the series features photographs, a chronology, two bibliographies, and a comprehensive index.

The History Makers series provides both students engaged in research and more casual readers with informative, enlightening, and entertaining overviews of individuals from a variety of circumstances, professions, and backgrounds. No doubt all of them, whether loved or hated, benevolent or cruel, constructive or destructive, will remain endlessly fascinating to each new generation seeking to identify the forces that shaped their world.

Greece's Pivotal Movers and Shakers

"Never in the history of the world has there been such a multiplication of varied talents and achievements within so limited a period," writes the noted classical historian Michael Grant.[1] He refers specifically to the leading figures in Greece's Classic Age, roughly encompassing the fifth and fourth centuries B.C. But the scope of his statement could easily be expanded to cover the century preceding and the century following the Classic Age. During these four centuries, a few hundred outstanding Greek lawgivers, political and military leaders, poets, dramatists, philosophers, sculptors, and painters created most of the major underpinnings of Western (European-based) culture and society. For more than twenty centuries, Greece has exerted "a peculiar enchantment" over the human imagination, comments another eminent scholar, C. M. Bowra:

> Even today . . . the Greek view of life excites and exalts us. Greek thought and Greek assumptions are closely woven into the fabric of our lives almost without our knowing it. . . . Ancient Greece left us some of the most magnificent works of art and literary monuments ever bequeathed by one civilization to another. But it is not mostly for these that the legacy of Greece is great. It is rather, because of the spirit they evoke, a spirit rooted in the belief that man is a free, indeed an exalted, being. . . . And for this reason alone we are right to wish to know about the Greeks, to assess the value and the scope of their achievement.[2]

Of the relatively small group of remarkable individuals who created the Greek legacy, this book focuses on the careers and accomplishments of eight political and military leaders. Each was either a guiding force behind or a direct participant in the crucial events of his time.

Shapers of the Greek Legacy

The first four of these men were Athenians. Though many Greek city-states produced talented, capable leaders, Athens was the largest, richest, and most influential state; for a long time its leaders either dominated or strongly influenced the affairs of other Greeks. The statesman Solon, for example, instituted important legal, political, and social reforms in the sixth century B.C. These reforms laid the foundations for Athens's establishment of the world's first democracy—a form of government that many other Greek states soon adopted—at the dawn of the fifth century and Classic Age.

The second Athenian examined is Themistocles, a shrewd early-fifth-century politician and military strategist. One of the key leaders of the Greek resistance to a massive invasion by the mighty Persian Empire, he played a central role in saving Greece, including Athens and its young democracy, from annihilation. Survival of the Persian threat

Themistocles, pictured in this likeness from later times, when Greece was under Roman rule, helped to expel the Persians in the fifth century B.C.

allowed his younger contemporary, the famous Athenian statesman Pericles, to continue to expand that democracy. Under Pericles' guidance, in the mid– to late fifth century Athens built an empire that influenced the fortunes of hundreds of city-states. During Pericles' time Athens also produced an artistic and literary cultural outburst unlike anything seen before or since. The fourth Athenian, the slippery politician and military general Alcibiades, was a key figure in the disastrous Peloponnesian War. This conflict engulfed almost all the Greek states and brought Athens's short-lived empire crashing down. Alcibiades' infamous betrayal of Athens was, arguably, a major cause of its decline and defeat.

In the two centuries following the great war, Athens was largely eclipsed by other Greek states. The fifth leader examined here, Epaminondas, was a brilliant military general who led his city-state, Thebes, to its brief but important mastery of Greece in the mid–fourth century B.C. His military innovations contributed to the success of the next two pivotal leaders—Philip and Alexander, the renowned father-and-son kings of Macedonia. Long a culturally backward kingdom of far northern Greece, Macedonia rose, under Philip, to dominate the Greek world. After Philip's untimely death in 336, Alexander embarked on a campaign of conquest that spread Greek language and culture throughout the Near East.

Alexander's empire collapsed after his own untimely death in 323. In the decades that followed, numerous military strongmen vied for control of the various Greek lands. One of the most powerful and talented of these men, Pyrrhus, king of the small Greek kingdom of Epirus, is the eighth leader here examined. He repeatedly fought, but could not decisively defeat, the Romans, whose power was then on the rise in the western Mediterranean. This early Greek-Roman conflict foreshadowed Rome's conquest of the Greek world in the following century.

The ideas, goals, and deeds of these eight men significantly affected the course of Greek political and social development. Some of them affected its cultural development too, if indirectly, by supporting the endeavors of creative people or championing and spreading Greek culture. Thus the diverse talents and abilities of Greek politicians, military generals, writers, artists, and philosophers com-

Alexander, who would later be called "the Great," pays his respects at the Temple of Apis in Memphis, Egypt.

bined to create the unique and indelible Greek legacy. "It was they, individually," Grant maintains, "who understood and shaped and transformed the world around them according to their personal wills."[3] Indeed, through Greece's profound legacy, the world still feels the power and endures the consequences of those wills.

CHAPTER 1

A Brief History of Ancient Greece

During the winter of 480–479 B.C., a large army of Persian troops camped in Thessaly, in central Greece, in preparation for a spring military campaign against the tiny city-states dotting southern Greece. Only months before, a small fleet of Greek warships had decisively defeated a much larger Persian fleet in the bay of Salamis, southwest of Athens. Afterward, the Persian king, Xerxes (pronounced ZERK-seez), had retired back into Asia. He had remained supremely confident, however, that his land army could and would crush the insolent Greeks; for that purpose he had left behind a large contingent of troops under the command of his son-in-law, Mardonius.

Left to his own devices, Mardonius reasoned that one way to ensure victory would be to persuade Athens, the largest Greek state, to join him against the other Greeks. To that end he sent an envoy to the Athenian leaders. According to the fifth-century B.C. Greek historian Herodotus, the envoy asked:

> Why are you so mad as to take up arms against the [Persian] king? You can never defeat him. . . . So stop trying to be a match for the king, at the cost of the loss of your country and continual peril of your lives. Come to terms with him instead. . . . Make an alliance with us.[4]

The Athenians promptly refused Mardonius's offer and then told some fellow Greeks that he had shown "a poor estimate of the spirit of Athens." There was not enough gold or fine land in all the world, the Athenians said, to induce them to betray their fellow Greeks. To be sure, it was not national loyalty they were expressing, for at the time Greece was not a single nation in the modern sense; it was rather a collection of small city-states, each of which saw itself as a nation unto itself. More often than not these states squabbled and warred among themselves. By refusing to join the Persians, the Athenians were defending a more fundamental ideal.

It was, in their own words, "the community of blood and language, temples and ritual; our common way of life; if Athens were to betray all this, it would not be well done."[5]

What *was* well done was the impressive, if temporary, display of unity by Athens and most of its neighbors against the foreign foe. The following summer the Greeks so decisively mauled Mardonius's army that the Persians never again risked invading Europe. Buoyed with a newfound confidence in their own abilities, the major Greek states, most especially Athens, set in motion the brief but magnificent cultural renaissance that has awed the world ever since.

Tourists congregate around the spectacular Lion Gate at Mycenae, a Bronze Age fortress located in the northeastern Peloponnesus.

Who were these defiant and talented Greeks, who shared a common culture, saved Europe from Persian domination, and created so many of the political, military, artistic, and philosophical concepts that have influenced the Western world for more than two thousand years? Where did they come from? How did they rise to greatness? And what caused their eventual demise?

Greece in the Bronze Age

The search for the answers to these questions begins long ago in the Bronze Age. This was the era in southern Europe (ca. 3000–1100 B.C.) when people used tools and weapons made of bronze, an alloy of copper and tin. Experts find it difficult to determine exactly when Greek-speaking people arrived in mainland Greece. As Thomas Martin, a scholar at Holy Cross, phrases it:

At what point in time does it make sense to use the term *Greeks* to refer to the inhabitants of the region called Greece? No simple answer will do. The process by which Greeks became Greeks does not lend itself to easy categorization because the concept of identity encompasses not just basic social and material conditions but also ethnic, cultural, and linguistic traditions.[6]

Archaeological evidence shows that people speaking an early form of Greek inhabited mainland Greece in the mid–second millennium B.C. They are referred to as Mycenaeans, after their chief fortress-town of Mycenae (in the northeastern part of the Peloponnesus, the large peninsula that makes up the southern third of Greece). Scholars are unsure, but the best guess is that the Mycenaeans entered Greece in two or more waves, beginning about 2000 B.C.[7] The Mycenaeans, says C. M. Bowra, "were spectacular builders. Their palaces were built within formidable citadels with walls 10 feet thick, and some of their royal tombs were enormous beehive structures made of stones weighing, sometimes, as much as 120 tons."[8]

For a long time the Mycenaeans came under the cultural influence, and perhaps also to some degree the military domination, of the Minoans, a highly civilized non-Greek-speaking people inhabiting Crete and other Aegean islands. This situation may be the basis for the well-known myth of Theseus, in which Cretan overlords periodically demanded and got supplies of sacrificial victims from the mainland city of Athens.[9] Whatever their relationship with the people on the mainland, the Minoans built huge, splendid palaces of their own (featuring highly advanced facilities, such as flush toilets and hot and cold running water) and carried on a prosperous trade with Egyptian and Near Eastern cities.

The Trojan War and Homeric Epics

For reasons that are still unclear, by about 1400 B.C. Minoan power had declined enough to allow Mycenaean warlords to take over the Cretan world.[10] For the next two centuries, the Mycenaeans prospered. They apparently frequently raided the coasts of Asia Minor (or Anatolia, now Turkey); one of these expeditions turned out to be the most important event in their history (at least as it relates to later Greek history). At some point between 1250 and 1200, they attacked and burned Troy, an independent trading city on Asia Minor's northwestern coast.

The sprawling ruins of the Minoan palace at Knossus, in northern Crete, were excavated in the early years of the twentieth century.

The memory of the Trojan War was preserved in oral traditions and later became the basis for the *Iliad* and *Odyssey*, epic poems attributed to the legendary eighth-century poet Homer. The importance of these epics to the later Greeks, especially in the Classic Age, cannot be overstated. Their leading characters, including the larger-than-life heroes Achilles, Hector, and Odysseus, interacted with the gods in what was seen as a glorious past age. In fact, the later Greeks referred to that legendary era, what we call the late Bronze Age, as the "Age of Heroes." Most of the important Greek myths originated in that era and a good many of them revolved around Mycenaean cities and culture. More significantly, as Michael Grant explains, the Homeric poems

> supplied the Greeks with their greatest civilizing influence, and formed the foundation of their literary, artistic, moral, social, educational, and political attitudes. . . . They attracted universal esteem and reverence, too, as sources of general and practical wisdom, as arguments for heroic yet human nobility and dignity, as incentives to vigorous . . . manly action, and as mines of endless quotations and commentaries: the common property of Greeks everywhere.[11]

The Dark Age and Birth of City-States

Not long after Troy's fall, perhaps about 1200 B.C. or shortly thereafter, the Aegean region, as well as many parts of the Near

Minoan trade wares rest in their original positions in the Bronze Age town of Akrotiri, on the Aegean island of Thera.

During the Greek Dark Age, most Mycenaean settlements, including Mycenae, shown here, fell into permanent ruin.

East, underwent a period of unprecedented upheaval. Most of the major Mycenaean strongholds were sacked and burned, never to be rebuilt. Many theories—civil conflicts, economic collapse, invasion by tribal peoples migrating from the north and east—have been advanced to explain the demise of Mycenaean civilization.[12] Regardless of whether one or a combination of these factors caused the catastrophe, apparently the only mainland city that survived intact was Athens. But in time even there, as in the rest of Greece, writing, record keeping, large-scale political organization, and other aspects of advanced civilization all but vanished. Greece slipped into what is now referred to as its Dark Age (ca. 1100–800 B.C.), a period about which scholars know very little.

In the Dark Age, the Minoan-Mycenaean world steadily passed into legend and the surviving Greeks (including any invaders who had recently settled the area) more or less forgot their heritage. Poverty was widespread and most people probably made a meager living from whatever fish they could catch, animals they could raise, or crops they could grow.[13] Small groups of people began identifying themselves only with the particular isolated valley or island where they lived; as time went on, these settlements became the bases for new political-social units commonly described as city-states. The Greeks called the city-state the polis (or, when plural, poleis).

Typically, each polis consisted of a central town surrounded by small villages and farmland; the town was built around a hill or cliff called an acropolis, which means "the city's high place" in Greek. The city's inhabitants fortified their acropolis to defend against attackers. But though the majority of city-states shared

By the Archaic Age, many Greeks thought that Bronze Age ruins like this Mycenaean tomb had been constructed by mythological giants.

some physical similarities, they developed differing systems of government and traditions and came to think of themselves as tiny separate nations. Still, as the Athenians later told the Persian envoy, all Greeks felt linked by their common language, religious beliefs and rituals, and myths from the Age of Heroes.

Farmers and Fighters in the Archaic Age

As many city-states grew increasingly prosperous, Greece steadily rose from its backward state. In what historians call the Archaic Age (ca. 800–500 B.C.), trade and commerce revived, and reading and writing reappeared (this time using an alphabet borrowed from the Phoenicians, a Near Eastern trading people). Local populations expanded, prompting several cities to establish colonies along the shores of the Aegean, Black, and Mediterranean Seas.

There was also much experimentation with systems of government. Power was originally in the hands of aristocrats (from the Greek word *aristoi,* meaning "best people"). But beginning in the mid-600s, ambitious individuals in several leading cities exploited the common people's antiaristocratic feelings to place themselves in power. The Greeks came to call these men, who were essentially petty dictators, tyrants. The negative meaning of the term tyrant, an "oppressive leader," developed later; in the beginning at least, a number of tyrants upheld most local laws, supported the arts, and enjoyed wide popular support. But as a form of government tyranny was short-lived in Greece. This is because a tyrant needed popular support, especially from his community's soldiers, to stay in power; the citizen bodies of many city-states, which included the soldiers, increasingly came to eliminate the tyrants and to assume the duties of governing themselves.

This trend toward democratic government was part of an ongoing revolution in agriculture and warfare that had begun in Greece's Dark Age. Noted classical scholar Victor D. Hanson calls it "an enormous transformation . . . nothing less than the creation of an entire class, which through sheer preponderance of numbers overwhelmed" the aristocratic rulers.[14] This class, unlike any the world had yet seen, was made up of tough, independent farmers who neither needed nor wanted control by aristocratic or other ruling elites. (By contrast, the Mycenaeans had practiced a collective form of agriculture, in which farmers were poor peasants controlled and exploited by the state.) Expressions of human freedom and individualism in Greek poetry and philosophy in the Archaic Age, says Hanson, were "manifestations of an ongoing and radically new private approach to rural life, and farming in particular."[15]

This class of independent farmers became not only the economic backbone of the typical polis, but also the source of its military strength. The practice of individual farmers, and later small communities of farmers, taking up arms to protect their lands, private property, and heritage against aggressors steadily led to the development of citizen militias. By the seventh century B.C., well-organized military units and tactics had developed, built around heavily armored infantry soldiers called hoplites (possibly after their large round shield, the *hoplon*), who wielded thrusting spears and short swords. They fought in a special formation

17

known as a phalanx, most often composed of eight ranks, or rows, of soldiers. When standing in close order, their uplifted shields created a formidable unbroken protective barrier. As the formation marched toward an enemy, the men in the front rank jabbed their spears at their opponents, while the hoplites in the rear ranks pushed at their comrades' backs, giving the whole unit a tremendous and lethal forward momentum. The members of local phalanxes, full-time farmers and part-time but highly effective fighters, Hanson states, "helped to establish agrarian control of the political life of their respective city-states." [16]

Athens Ascendant

Thus, it was only a matter of time before agrarian ideals of freedom and independence were translated into political ones. The slow but steady movement toward democracy in Greece reached its first and greatest expression in Athens in the late sixth and early fifth centuries B.C., the dawn of the Classic Age. Building on the earlier and significant legal, social, and political reforms of the statesman Solon, in about 508 a popular leader named Cleisthenes spearheaded the creation of complete citizen control of government. In the years that followed, other reformers, most notably the statesmen Ephialtes (died 461) and Pericles (died 429) expanded the Athenian democracy; and many other poleis followed Athens's lead and instituted their own versions of democratic government.

This late-fourth-century B.C. terra-cotta painting of a hoplite is now on display in Athens's Acropolis Museum.

During these same years, Athens acquired great power and prestige and came to dominate international affairs in the Greek world, in part because it was the largest, most populous, and wealthiest polis in Greece.[17] Another important factor in its ascendancy was the leading role it played in defending against the back-to-back Persian invasions of the early fifth century. In 490, an army sent by Persia's King Darius landed at Marathon, northeast of Athens. There, a tiny force of Athenian hoplites decisively defeated the invaders, gaining for Athens the image among a majority of Greeks

The Parthenon, constructed in honor of Athens's patron goddess, looms atop the Athenian Acropolis, seen from the southwest.

as their savior. When Darius's son, Xerxes, launched another invasion a decade later, Athens once more took the lead, as its skilled politician and admiral, Themistocles, largely engineered the Greek naval victory at Salamis.

After the defeat of the Persians in 479, Athens headed an alliance of over a hundred city-states, the original purpose of which was to protect Greece from further Persian invasions. Over time, however, the Athenians transformed the alliance into their own very lucrative maritime empire. Under the direction of Pericles, the dominant Greek political figure of the mid–fifth century, much of the wealth that flowed into Athens's coffers went into public construction projects designed to beautify the city and make it the wonder and envy of Greece. This goal was achieved with the creation of a magnificent temple complex (begun in the 440s) atop the Athenian acropolis, crowned by the famous Parthenon (temple of Athena, Athens's patron goddess). These monuments became a marvel not only to the Greeks of that time, but to all succeeding generations. Over five centuries later, they inspired this comment from the Greek biographer and moralist Plutarch:

> It is this, above all, which makes Pericles' works an object of wonder to us—the fact that they were created in so short a span, and yet for all time. Each one possessed a beauty which seemed venerable [impressive in old age] the moment it was born, and at the same time a youthful vigor which makes them appear to this day as if they were newly built. A bloom of eternal freshness hovers over these works of his and preserves them from the touch of time.[18]

19

Incessant Warfare Leads to Decline

But the ambitious and energetic Athenians were unable to maintain the momentum that had propelled them to the heights of power and glory. In large part this was the result of a long-standing rivalry with Sparta, a city-state located in the southern Peloponnesus. Athens had Greece's strongest navy, but Sparta, with a highly regimented social and political life built around military training, possessed its most formidable land army. Each of the two states was convinced that it alone should enjoy supremacy in Greece; after many decades of mutual distrust and small-scale fighting, each finally reached a point at which it was willing to wage a major war to gain that supremacy.

Ionic columns grace the ruins of the Erechtheum, a temple situated on the northern side of the Acropolis.

The result of this rivalry was the Peloponnesian War (so named because Sparta and its major allies resided in the Peloponnesus), which erupted in 431 B.C. In the words of Thucydides, the contemporary Greek historian who chronicled the war,

> If both sides nourished the boldest hopes and put forth their utmost strength for the war, this was only natural. Zeal is always at its height at the commencement of an undertaking; and on this particular occasion the Peloponnesus and Athens were both full of young men whose inexperience made them eager to take up arms, while the rest of Greece stood straining with excitement at the conflict of its leading cities.[19]

The "rest of Greece" ended up doing more than watching from the sidelines, however. The conflict inevitably drew in most of the city-states, who aligned themselves in two blocs, one led by Athens, the other by Sparta. And the eagerness to fight that so many had expressed early on eventually turned to regret and lament. In a scenario no one expected, the war dragged on for twenty-seven grueling years and ultimately proved ruinous for all involved. Athens went down to defeat in 404, ending its golden age and hegemony (dominance) of Greece, and for a short time even losing its cherished democracy.

Following the great war, the Greek city-states entered a period of political and military decline. Not only had the conflict caused widespread death and destruction, but its combatants had failed to learn from it the lesson that continued disunity and rivalry was futile and dangerous. At first, because of its victory over Athens, Sparta dominated Greek affairs. But the Spartans failed to maintain their hegemony of Greece, partly because they were not able administrators. Also, they were insensitive and heavy-handed in their dealings with other city-states. In 382 B.C., for example, Spartan troops sent to stop a civil conflict in Thebes seized that city's acropolis and initiated a brutal military occupation that most Greeks heartily condemned. Athens responded to this and other Spartan aggressions by cultivating another bloc of its own allies; and soon the two sides were at each other's throats again.

But it was not Athens that was fated to humble the Spartan bully. Led by two talented and popular statesmen-generals, Pelopidas and Epaminondas, Thebes overhauled its military and surprised everyone by crushing Sparta's phalanx in a pivotal battle in 371. This helped to end the Spartan hegemony and to initiate a Theban one.

Thebes did not enjoy its position of power and influence for long, however. Less than a decade later, the Thebans fought a major battle against an unlikely, and decidedly temporary, coalition led by Athens and Sparta. Afterwards, according to the Athenian historian Xenophon (pronounced ZEN-uh-phon), "There was even more uncertainty and confusion in Greece . . . than there had been previously."[20]

The Rise of Macedonia

Decades of bickering, war, and shifting political alliances had left the major mainland city-states exhausted, weakened, and therefore vulnerable to outside attack. But this time the threat came not from Asia, as it had

The ruins of the marketplace (agora) at Thasos, an island member of the alliance that Athens transformed into an empire.

in the previous century, but rather from their own backyard, so to speak. The tribes of Macedonia, a kingdom in extreme northern Greece, had long been disunited and militarily weak. The city-state Greeks had generally viewed them contemptuously as uncultured backwoods types inhabiting the periphery of the civilized world and for the most part had ignored them.

This turned out to be a grave mistake. In the mid–fourth century B.C., just as Theban power was on the decline and exhaustion and confusion reigned in southern Greece, a brilliant and capable young man—Philip II—ascended the Macedonian throne. In an amazingly short time, he brought his land's disunited tribes together, forming a strong nation with a powerful army. Philip eventually set his sights on becoming master of all of Greece; after years of on-and-off negotiations, treaties signed and ignored, cities besieged, and territories seized, he accomplished that goal. In 338, he and his then teenaged son, Alexander III (born 356), decisively defeated a united Greek army led by Athens and Thebes, and Philip assumed the title of "Captain General" of Greece.

When Philip was assassinated two years later, Alexander carried on his father's plans, which included an invasion of the Persian Empire. In 334, Alexander crossed the Hellespont (the narrow strait

22

This first-century Roman mosaic depicts Alexander the Great at the Battle of Issus, one of his victories over the Persians.

separating northern Greece from Asia Minor) at the head of a small but, as it turned out, very powerful army. In just ten years, he conquered the vast Persian domain, and in the process spread Greek language and culture to many parts of the Near East. In 323, however, he died unexpectedly, leaving his leading generals to fight over his newly acquired empire.

The Hellenistic Age and the Fall of Greece

And fight they did, for a very long time. For over forty years, in fact, these men, who came to be called the *Diadochi* ("successors"), and their sons, the *Epigoni* ("those born after"), waged war among themselves until three major new Greek kingdoms emerged. The Ptolemaic Kingdom consisted mainly of Egypt and parts of nearby Palestine; the Seleucid Kingdom encompassed the lands north and west of the Persian Gulf—the heart of the old Persian Empire—and parts of Asia Minor; and the Macedonian Kingdom was made up mostly of Macedonia and the Greek mainland. Historians refer to these realms collectively as Hellenistic, meaning "Greek-like," since their cultures often consisted of a fusion of Greek and various Eastern languages, customs, and ideas. (Likewise, the period lasting from Alexander's death in 323 B.C. to the death of the last Hellenistic ruler, Cleopatra VII, in 31 B.C., is called the Hellenistic Age.)

The Hellenistic states ended up repeating the same fatal mistake the city-states had; they argued and fought among themselves,

23

creating disunity, weakness, and vulnerability to outside aggressors. In the mid–third century B.C., as they squabbled, far to the west the Romans, masters of the Italian peninsula, were entering their first war against the maritime empire of Carthage, centered in Tunisia, in North Africa. Shortly before, one of the Hellenistic rulers, Pyrrhus of Epirus, had briefly fought the Romans. The fact that he, one of the greatest Greek generals of that or any day, could not decisively defeat them did not bode well for the future of either Carthage or Greece. In 213, a Greek orator, Agelaus of Aetolia, recognized the potential danger and warned:

> It would be best of all if the Greeks never went to war with one another, if they could regard it as the greatest gift of the gods for them to speak with one voice, and could join hands like men who are crossing a river; in this way they could unite to repulse the incursions of the barbarians [non-Greek-speaking peoples] and to preserve themselves and their cities. . . . For it must already be obvious to all those who pay even the slightest attention to affairs of state that whether the Carthaginians defeat the Romans or the Romans the Carthaginians, the victors will by no means be satisfied with the sovereignty of Italy and Sicily, but will come here, and will advance both their forces and their ambitions beyond the bounds of justice.[21]

But Agelaus's warning went unheeded. Rome went on to annihilate Carthage and soon afterward began picking off the Hellenistic kingdoms one by one. By 168 the Romans had absorbed the Macedonian realm. In 64 they dismantled the last remnants of the Seleucid Kingdom (the region occupied by modern Syria), turning them into a province. And in 31 they defeated Cleopatra, last of the Ptolemies (the line of rulers descended from Alexander's general, Ptolemy), at Actium, in western Greece. The seas where for centuries Greek cargo vessels and warships had held sway, and indeed the entire Mediterranean world, had become, in the words of noted historian Naphtali Lewis, "a Roman lake, and those who lived on and around it looked to Rome as the arbiter of their fortunes."[22]

The Romans were mightily impressed and influenced by Greek culture, and by absorbing much of it they ensured that the Greek cultural legacy would survive. However, largely because the ancient Greeks never achieved the greater strength that would have come from the "one voice" of unity, independent Greek rule vanished from the world for over nineteen centuries.

CHAPTER 2

Solon: Lawgiver and Social Reformer

To the mass of the people I gave the power they needed,
Neither degrading them, nor giving them too much rein.
For those who already possessed great power and wealth
I saw to it that their interests were not harmed.
I stood guard with a broad shield before both parties
And prevented either from triumphing unjustly.[23]

These are probably the most famous lines written by Solon, the first Athenian poet and earliest Greek statesman whose own words have survived the ravages of time. The "parties" before whom he held the "broad shield" of protection and justice were classes of rich and poor Athenians, whose long-standing disagreements and mutual contempt had, by the early sixth century B.C., brought the polis to the brink of open civil strife. By creating broad-based political and social reforms, Solon saved Athens from destructive class warfare. These reforms, including a new legal code, also laid the foundations for the city's democracy, which would emerge at the end of the century under other enlightened reformers.

Solon's efforts to relieve tensions between economic classes and improve the quality of life in Athens drew mixed reactions at the time. But later generations of Athenians and other Greeks praised them highly. They came to revere his memory and ranked him as one of the Seven Sages, larger-than-life figures widely viewed as the wisest men Greece had produced.[24]

Solon's Early Years

Plutarch (who wrote during the late first and early second centuries A.D.) and the fourth-century B.C. philosopher-scholar Aristotle recorded Solon's principal deeds and preserved some of his writings. But they had little to say about his background and personal life, which therefore remain obscure. He was likely born about 630 B.C.

into a well-to-do aristocratic Athenian family. According to Plutarch, Solon's father, Execestides, claimed descent from one of Athens's early kings, and his mother was a cousin of the mother of Pisistratus, who later became Athens's first tyrant. The fact that Solon and Pisistratus were kinsmen partly explains why, even when they later pursued opposing political policies, they remained on friendly terms.

One of several later speculative depictions of the Athenian statesman Solon. No one knows what he actually looked like.

Nothing is known about Solon's childhood, but as a young adult he apparently became a merchant of modest means. This was unusual at the time, for aristocrats traditionally made their money by exploiting the land they owned and almost never got directly involved in the details of buying and selling, which they saw as beneath their station. Plutarch records two traditions that supposedly explain why Solon chose the life of a traveling merchant:

> Solon's father . . . dissipated a great deal of his estate in various acts of charity, but there was no lack of [rich] friends who would have been ready to help his son. Solon, however, coming as he did of a family which had always been accustomed to give help to others, was ashamed to accept any for himself, and so while he was still a young man, he ventured into commerce. On the other hand, we are also told that he traveled to gain experience and to extend his knowledge rather than to make money.[25]

Perhaps in his late twenties or early thirties Solon first distinguished himself as a public figure among his countrymen. The evidence is skimpy and unclear, but it appears that he played an important role in an ongoing Athenian dispute with the city-state of Megara, located about thirty miles west of Athens. About the time of Solon's birth, Athens and Megara began fighting off and on for possession of the island of Salamis, lying almost directly south of Megara's urban center. In the decades that followed, Athens may have gained and then lost the island one or more times.[26] Solon wrote a patriotic poem urging his fellow Athenians to continue (or resume?) the struggle, saying: "Let us go to Salamis, that we may do battle for the lovely island, and fling off our bitter disgrace." [27] The problem is that the date of the poem is uncertain and he may have written it after he was already famous. Similarly, traditional stories claiming that he commanded a military force that successfully captured the island may be later inventions.

Whatever the nature of the deeds he performed, by circa 594 B.C., the year that Solon first held high office, he was widely respected throughout the thousand-square-mile Athenian territory of Attica as a wise and fair-minded man who deeply loved his country. It was, evidently, his strong sense of justice that motivated his countrymen in that year to seek his aid in averting a civil war.

Long-Standing Injustice Leads to Crisis

The social-political disputes Solon was asked to mediate were rooted in the city's dim past. At some unknown date, Athens's early kings had been replaced by public administrators called archons, of which there were originally three. At first one or more of these served for life, but sometime in the early seventh century B.C. annual elections began. By the middle of that century, six more archons had been added, for a total of nine. It remains somewhat unclear who chose them, but most scholars believe they were elected by the Assembly (*Ecclesia*), a group of Athenian landholders who met mainly for this purpose. Probably the Assembly had few, if any, other powers at this time.

The archons were all aristocrats and when they left office they became lifetime members of the Areopagus, a council that, tradition held, the gods had created. The amount of power the aristocratic Areopagus wielded in this period is unclear. But it seems certain that it at least advised the archons and functioned as a law court. Aristotle later claimed that it did much more, and often in an oppressive manner:

> The Council of Areopagus had the official function of guarding the laws, but actually it administered the greatest number and the most important of the affairs of state, inflicting penalties and fines upon offenders against public order without appeal. [28]

As time went on the common people increasingly came to resent the stranglehold the nobles held on government and public affairs. Shortly before Solon was born, a prominent aristocrat named Cylon assaulted the Acropolis and tried to make himself tyrant in Athens. The coup failed, mainly because farmers and other commoners armed themselves and killed Cylon's followers.

The incident demonstrated not only the high degree of popular unrest, but also the formidable threat that Athens's citizen soldiers posed to the ruling aristocrats.

It was clear that the people wanted reform. And the nobles took a tentative step in that direction by appointing one of the members of the Areopagus, Draco (or Dracon), to create a written law code. However, Draco's laws were so harsh that most Athenians came to see them as "written in blood rather than ink." Moreover, Draco did nothing to stop the increasingly common practice of debt bondage. Wealthy landowners had a number of poor tenant farmers living and working on their estates. The dependent tenants, and also some of the poorest independent farmers, periodically sought loans from the prosperous owners, especially in years when harvests were bad. When a poor borrower could not pay back his loan, the owner was allowed to recover his investment by selling him, as well as members of his family, into slavery.

This unjust and cruel practice eventually drove the poor to the brink of revolt. And they were not alone. The better-off independent farmers and other members of the middle class, who made up the bulk of Athens's hoplite militia (the group that had foiled

A meeting of the Areopagus, an aristocratic council that served as a law court and may for a while have wielded much power.

28

This nineteenth-century engraving depicts Solon dictating his laws, which were far less repressive than those enacted in the previous century.

Cylon's coup), were dissatisfied and angry that they were still largely excluded from government. By the early 500s B.C., the possibility of these two discontented groups joining forces and violently overthrowing the ruling order was a genuine threat. This was the serious and unstable situation the various factions asked Solon, whom they all trusted, to deal with in 594.

The Laws Reformed

Perhaps to make Solon's mediation as official as possible, his countrymen made him archon. Interestingly, many on both sides thought this position was not powerful enough, given the importance of the task at hand, and urged him to establish himself as tyrant. As Plutarch says, "They were by no means unwilling to have a single man, the justest and wisest in the state, placed at the head of affairs." [29] But Solon showed that he was indeed wise by refusing to become dictator; for it was the amassing of too much power in the hands of a few that had caused the very problems he had been asked to solve. Supposedly he said, "If I could get the mastery, and seize boundless wealth and the lordship of Athens for one single day, I would be willing afterwards to be flayed [skinned] for a wineskin [leather pouch], and let my family be obliterated." [30]

Solon also demonstrated his sense of justice, as well as his courage, by immediately enacting a major reform that was sure to upset the aristocrats, namely the complete elimination of debt bondage. According to Aristotle:

Solon having become master of affairs made the people free both at the time and for the future by prohibiting loans secured on the person, and he laid down laws, and enacted cancellations of debts both private and public, the measures that are known as "the Shaking-off of Burdens" [*Seisachtheia*], meaning that the people shook off their load.[31]

As one of Solon's own writings attests, he also arranged for the reuniting of many families that had suffered under the former unjust system:

This fanciful European painting of Solon explaining his laws to his countrymen depicts them in an eighteenth-century setting.

Many people I restored to Athens, their native city divinely-founded, who . . . had been sold abroad, and others who through pressure of need had gone into exile, and who through wanderings far and wide no longer spoke the Attic tongue [i.e., the Athenian version of the Ionian dialect of Greek].[32]

Solon also eliminated Draco's repressive laws, except for those dealing with homicide. In what evidently constituted the only progressive aspects of his code, Draco had differentiated between murder and manslaughter (unpremeditated murder), setting a penalty of exile, rather than death, for the latter. While retaining these murder laws, Solon added a new and controversial reform. He forbade families to enact "blood-vengeance," or capturing and punishing murderers on their own, and required them to begin legal proceedings first.

Balancing the Old and the New

Next, Solon turned his attention to the area of political rights. To eliminate the nobles' monopoly on government and give the common people a greater political voice, he introduced a sweeping new system of social ranking. He ordered that a census be taken, and based on its results divided the people into four classes according to their income (reckoned in *medimnoi*, or large bushels, of grain or the equivalent in other produce). According to Plutarch:

> Those who received an annual income of 500 bushels or more of wet or dry produce, he placed in the first class and called them *Pentakosiomedimnoi* [literally, "five-hundred-bushel-men"]. The second class consisted of men who could afford a horse, or possessed an income of 300 [to 500] bushels, and these, because they paid a "horse tax," were known as Knights [*Hippeis*]. The third class were the *Zeugitai* [farmers], whose yearly income amounted to 200 [to 300] bushels. . . . The rest of the citizen body [earning less than the equivalent of 200 bushels] were known as *Thetes* [laborers].[33]

The importance of this new social division was that it provided political opportunities and rights to many who before had had few or none. Although a majority of those in the highest class were still aristocrats, any number of commoners could now join them, since wealth, rather than birth, had become the requirement for entry. As Michael Grant comments, Solon's imposition of timocracy (rule by the wealthy) "created the concept of an impersonal state, as opposed to arbitrary noble leadership."[34] The new system also allowed the nonlandowning laborers in the lowest class to attend and vote in the Assembly, making that body more democratic. Clearly, the practice of filling public offices with wealthy aristocrats chosen by wealthy landowners had ended.

A view of the Pnyx Hill, site of the meetings of the Athenian Assembly, which became more democratic and influential thanks to Solon.

Another of Solon's democratic reforms was the creation of the *Boule*, or Council, made up of four hundred citizens, one hundred from each of Athens's four ancient tribes.[35] The members were chosen by lot (random drawing) from all classes except the lowest and served for one year. Because the Council prepared the agenda for the discussions and voting that took place in the Assembly, the new body was very influential; its mostly nonaristocratic members served to balance the power of the aristocratic political advisers and judges who sat in the Areopagus, which Solon retained. "Solon had shown himself to be the archetypal [model] man of compromise," says Grant. "This very act of holding the balance between [the] old and new [systems] had given prominence to the new, reaching out towards a future political philosophy within which democratic institutions could grow." [36]

Public Reaction

All Athenians agreed that Solon's compromises and reforms had saved the state from slipping into political chaos and civil strife. But though some felt that he had fairly addressed the needs and rights of people in all classes, many were unhappy with the new system. "The rich," Plutarch writes,

> were angry at being deprived of their securities, and the poor even more so, because Solon did not carry out a redistribution of the land, as they had expected, or impose a strictly equal and uniform style of living upon everybody. . . . People came to visit him every day . . . finding fault with [one or more of his laws], or advising him to insert a certain provision here or to take out another there. A great many wanted to ask questions and cross-examine him on points of detail, and they kept pressing him to explain what was the object of this or that regulation. [37]

Some surviving verses by Solon suggest that he was at least a bit indignant and hurt by this reaction. But for his efforts, he wrote,

> the people—if I must utter my rebuke publicly—would never in their dreams have beheld the boons which they now hold. . . . For if another man [had held this office] he would not have checked the people, not have stopped before he had stirred up the milk and extracted the fatness [i.e., reaped some personal profit at the people's expense]. But I took my stand like a boundary-stone in the debatable land between the two parties. [38]

Old but Still Respected

Solon finally decided that, to escape the complainers and maintain what popularity he still had, it was best that he leave Athens for a

Solon may eventually have become an adviser to Pisistratus (on right in chariot), one of his younger relatives, who became Athens's tyrant.

while. For an unknown number of years he traveled around the eastern Mediterranean, visiting both Cyprus and Lydia (in Asia Minor). According to Plato, he also spent time in Egypt, where some local priests told him about the legend of the lost city of Atlantis and claimed that the Athenians were "descended from a small seed or remnant of them who survived" when it sank into the sea.[39]

It remains uncertain when Solon returned to Athens, but both Aristotle and Plutarch say that he was there when his kinsman Pisistratus made himself tyrant circa 561 B.C. This was one of the extreme political outcomes that Solon had sought to prevent in his reforms years before. Now very old, yet still a highly respected public figure, he supposedly became an adviser to Pisistratus before dying a year or two later. It is possible that Pisistratus's subsequent, largely benign rule and the survival of most of Solon's laws and political apparatus during that rule were due in some degree to Solon's influence on the dictator.

Solon's laws and political institutions, forming the base on which Cleisthenes and others would later build the world's first democracy, constitute part of the proof that Solon was an uncommonly just and wise man. Evidence of his wisdom also survives in his poetry, including the following "Ten Ages in the Life of Man." Its similarity to "The Seven Ages of Man" by a later poet of uncommon wisdom, William Shakespeare, is striking.

A boy who is still a child grows baby teeth and loses them
all in seven years.
When God makes him fourteen, the signs of maturity
begin to shine on his body.
In the third seven, limbs growing, chin bearded, his skin
acquires the color of manhood.
In the fourth age a man is at a peak in strength—a sign of
man in excellence.
The time is ripe in the fifth [age] for a young man to think
of marriage and of offspring.
In the sixth [age] the mind of man is trained in all things;
he doesn't try the impossible.
In the seventh and eighth [ages], that is, fourteen years, he
speaks most eloquently in his life.
He can still do much in the ninth [age] but his speech and
thought are discernibly less keen;
And if he makes the full measure of ten sevens, when death
comes, it will not come too soon.[40]

CHAPTER 3

Themistocles: Father of Athenian Naval Supremacy

In all of Athens's history, and in all of Greece in the fifth century B.C., no other figure was as pivotal as Themistocles, except, perhaps, for Pericles, architect of Athens's golden age. It was Themistocles, a shrewd and far-thinking politician, statesman, and admiral, who convinced the Athenians that their future lay in naval power; it was with the ships he built and commanded that the Greeks defeated the Persian armada at Salamis in 480 B.C., saving Greece from conquest; and it was those same ships that Athens used to begin building its maritime empire soon afterward. Moreover, at a time when many Athenian leaders sought to befriend Sparta, Themistocles correctly foresaw that the Spartans posed as much or more of a threat to Athens than the Persians had and took steps to fortify his city against future Spartan attacks.

It is important to realize that many of these accomplishments did not seem so remarkable to many of Themistocles' contemporaries. At the time, most of his ideas and deeds were controversial and he had many enemies, who eventually branded him, unjustly, as a traitor to his country. His tragedy was that he was too far ahead of his time, for only after his death was his triumph revealed. With the advantage of hindsight, many Greeks came to realize that his policies had made Athens's rise to greatness possible (although others remained convinced that he had been a traitor). In the late fifth century B.C., for example, Thucydides wrote:

> Themistocles was a man who exhibited the most indubitable signs of genius; indeed, in this particular he has a claim on our admiration quite extraordinary and unparalleled. . . . He was at once the best judge in those sudden crises which admit of little or of no deliberation, and the

best prophet of the future, even to its most distant possibilities. An able [theorist] . . . he was not without the power of passing an adequate judgment in matters in which he had no experience. He could also excellently divine the good and evil which lay hidden in the unseen future. To sum up . . . this extraordinary man . . . surpassed all others in . . . meeting an emergency.[41]

The Need for Family Connections

Themistocles' origins and early years are obscure. He was born about 523 B.C. in an Attic district located just northeast of Athens.

Themistocles, as he may have looked as a young man in hoplite gear.

All that is known about his father is the man's name—Neocles—but this in itself may be revealing. Neocles means "new fame," which suggests that he managed to gain some kind of respected position in the community but did not belong to the class of landed aristocrats. According to most later ancient writers, Themistocles' mother was a foreigner, from Thrace (a region of northern Greece) or Asia Minor. Some claimed she was a slave, but this is most likely a false story his political enemies created in hopes of discrediting him.[42]

In any case, as Plutarch says, Themistocles' family "was too obscure to have lent him any distinction at the beginning of his career."[43] He early set his sights on becoming successful in politics but had to contend with the reality that such success depended in large degree on one's family connections. Perhaps this is why as a young man (the exact date is unknown) he married Archippe, of the Alcmeonids, one of Athens's oldest and most prominent aristocratic families. It appears that she bore him five sons and three daughters.

It is probable that the family connection Themistocles most wanted to exploit by marrying into the Alcmeonid clan was the most illustrious of its recent members—Cleisthenes, principal creator of Athens's new democracy. Building on earlier reforms by the legendary lawgiver Solon, in 508 Cleisthenes "took the [common] people into his party," as Herodotus phrased it.[44] Although Solon's system had increased the political power of the middle and lower classes, aristocrats, like Cleisthenes himself, still largely ran the show. To win the support of the commoners, Cleisthenes greatly reduced aristocratic power and influence. He did this by replacing Athens's four traditional tribes, all controlled by noble houses, with ten new tribes, each of which featured a thorough mix of people from all social classes and operated, at least in theory, on the principle of social equality. He also increased the membership of the Council from four hundred to five hundred, fifty from each of the new tribes. The result was a radical and very popular form of direct democracy. By linking himself with the Alcmeonids about a decade or so later, Themistocles was likely able to cash in on the considerable prestige that Cleisthenes' name no doubt still carried among voters.

Themistocles as Archon

Whatever his means, Themistocles did manage to make an impressive name for himself in Athenian politics. The first firmly dated event in his career was his election to the office of chief archon in 493 B.C. This position not only gave him considerable political power during his year in office, but also ensured his continued influence as a permanent member of the prestigious Areopagus (which all archons joined at the end of their terms of service).

Even at this early date, Themistocles showed himself to be a man of vision. For centuries, the relatively open Phaleron Bay, located about five miles southwest of Athens, had served as the city's port. A strong advocate of the importance of naval power, he felt that the three natural harbors at Piraeus, a few miles farther up the coast, would be more practical and defensible. "Particularly the large northern harbor," writes one of his modern biographers, A. J. Podlecki,

> because of its shape like an inverted cup, he saw could be sufficiently fortified to withstand attacks by the enemy, foreign or Greek, and the further possibility may have occurred to him of linking the whole harbor complex with the upper city by a narrow, walled corridor, although this was not actually achieved until the fifties of the century.[45]

It is probable that Themistocles was worried about the growing Persian menace. Only about a year before he became archon, a Persian fleet had disastrously defeated the combined navies of the major Greek cities of Ionia (the Greek region running along the

37

western coast of Asia Minor); Miletus, the leading Ionian city, had been sacked, sending shock waves through the Greek world.[46] Sure enough, in 490 the Persians struck the Greek mainland at Marathon. By this time Themistocles was no longer archon, and Miltiades, chief general and victor at Marathon, had assumed leadership of Athens's anti-Persian resistance. Although Themistocles almost certainly fought at Marathon, possibly as one of Athens's ten elected generals, for the moment he remained in Miltiades' large political shadow.

Drawing Athens Down Toward the Sea

This situation changed markedly, however, only a year later. The Athenians tried, convicted, and fined Miltiades for deceiving them (after he led a failed military expedition against a Greek island that had collaborated with the Persians). After Miltiades' sudden fall from grace, the 480s B.C. witnessed several other popular leaders, Themistocles among them, opposing one another for political supremacy. Highlighting this intense rivalry was the frequent use of ostracism, a democratic practice akin to impeachment, in which citizens wrote the name of an official they wanted removed on broken pieces of pottery (called *ostraka*); if the official received six thousand or more of these negative votes, the city banished him for a period of ten years. Podlecki elaborates:

A restoration of Piraeus, Athens's port town, in the fifth century B.C., with the Athenian Acropolis visible in the distance at right.

The Athenians drive the Persians onto the beaches at Marathon, northeast of Athens, a battle in which Themistocles is believed to have fought.

It became a powerful weapon in the hands of a politician to secure temporary removal of an opponent so that his own proposals might proceed unobstructed. It was a relatively innocuous [harmless] penalty which did not involve confiscation of property or loss of citizen rights. . . . An ostracism did not just happen. Votes had to be canvassed by a man's opponents who saw to it that a sufficient number of citizens turned up to vote against him on ostracism day. In fact, a surprisingly large number of what appear to be prefabricated *ostraka* with Themistocles' name carefully inscribed on them have been unearthed to show that he himself was a near victim some time in the 480s.[47]

History has shown that it was fortunate for Athens that Themistocles emerged from this political warfare as one of Athens's two or three most influential public figures. He had long been convinced that Greece had not seen the last of the Persians. According to Plutarch:

The rest of the Athenians supposed that the Persian defeat at Marathon meant the end of the war. Themistocles, however, believed that it was only the prelude to a far greater struggle, and he prepared, as it were, to . . . put his city into training to meet it.[48]

In keeping with Themistocles' belief in the importance of naval power, this preparation and training mainly involved the construction

Themistocles' name figures prominently on this ostrakon, *now in Athens's Agora Museum. Many attempts were made to ostracize him.*

of new warships. At first, most Athenians did not favor the idea, partly because they did not yet believe that a new Persian assault was imminent. Also, building a whole fleet of ships and training their crews was a hugely expensive proposition. In this regard, Themistocles benefited from an unexpected stroke of luck. In 483, Athens's silver mines at Laurium produced the largest yield in recent memory, and as Herodotus says, the people (i.e., the voters in the Assembly),

> proposed to share out [the profits] amongst themselves at a rate of ten drachmas a man; Themistocles, however, persuaded them to give up this idea and, instead of distributing the money, to spend it on the construction of two hundred warships.[49]

This large naval buildup, along with Themistocles' completion of the fortifications at the port of Piraeus a few years later, prompted Plutarch's famous remark that "he continued to draw the Athenians little by little and to turn their thoughts in the direction of the sea."[50]

The Return of the Persians

No sooner had the new ships been built than it became clear to all Greeks that Themistocles' worries about the Persians' returning had been well founded. The invasion force that marched across Asia Minor toward the Hellespont in the spring of 480 B.C. dwarfed all others in ancient times. It consisted of an estimated 200,000 combat infantry and cavalry; 800 to 1,000 ships manned by at least 150,000 oarsmen and sailors; and a huge following of support personnel numbering perhaps as many as 300,000.[51]

As a wave of apprehension swept through Greece, the Athenians sought advice from the oracle at Delphi, in central Greece (a priestess who, it was thought, transmitted divine prophecies, although usually in vague or cryptic terms). Among other things, the oracle predicted that "the wooden wall only shall not fall, but help you and your children," and added, "divine Salamis, you will bring death to women's sons when the corn is scattered, or the harvest gathered in." [52] The Athenians were divided about the meaning of the "wooden wall." Many thought it referred to a wooden stockade that had once surrounded the Acropolis, suggesting that fortifying that central hill would protect the citizenry against the Persian horde. Themistocles, however, argued that the wooden wall was his large new fleet of ships, meaning that victory would be won at sea. Further, he held, the oracle's prediction of women's sons dying at Salamis referred to Persian, rather than Athenian, sons.[53]

Soon afterward, Themistocles met with leaders of neighboring city-states to plan a strategy to defend southern Greece against the advancing Persians. No doubt he argued that trying to fight Xerxes' huge land army was futile and that it would be far more realistic to concentrate their efforts on destroying the Persian fleet.

Pilgrims to Apollo's sacred shrine at Delphi look on as the oracle (priestess) swoons in preparation for delivering a divine message.

According to this view, without ships to supply and reinforce it, the Persian army would be far less effective.

By September 480, the Persians had entered southern Greece and were approaching Athens. While the Greek fleet prepared for the coming fight, Themistocles issued an emergency decree ordering Athens's evacuation:

> The city is to be entrusted to Athena, the guardian of Athens, and to all other gods for protection against the foreign enemy . . . [and as] for the Athenians themselves . . . children and women are to be taken to Troezen [on the Peloponnesian coast] . . . old men and slaves are to be taken to Salamis. . . . All other Athenians . . . of military age are to embark on the two hundred ships . . . and ward off the foreign enemy for the sake of freedom, both their own and that of the other Greeks.[54]

Themistocles' Finest Hour

On or about September 17, the Persians entered Athens, finding to their surprise that the city was largely deserted. The easy capture of the most famous polis in Greece must have elated King Xerxes; however, his brief occupation of an empty city turned out to be the high point of his campaign. For at that very moment, the Greek admirals were readying their fleets for battle. And this fateful juncture, in which the future of all Greece hung precariously in the balance, proved to be Themistocles' finest hour. The other admirals wanted to abandon Attica and take up a new defensive position at the Isthmus of Corinth, many miles to the south. But he vehemently insisted that the Greeks make their stand at Salamis, declaring:

Athens's Acropolis is visible in the distance at right in this view from the southeast. The Persians occupied the city in 480 B.C.

> It is now in your power to save Greece if you take my advice and engage the enemy's fleet here at Salamis, instead of withdrawing to the Isthmus. . . . If you fight there, it will have to be in the open sea, and that will be greatly to our disadvantage, with our smaller numbers. . . . [Whereas, at Salamis] we shall be fighting in narrow waters,

and there . . . we shall win. . . . Fighting in a confined space favors us but the open sea favors the enemy.

When the other commanders continued to oppose his plan, Themistocles grew angry and threatened:

If you refuse [to do as I say] we [i.e., the Athenians] will immediately put our families aboard [our ships] and sail for . . . Italy [and there establish a new city of Athens]. . . . Where will you be without the Athenian fleet? When you have lost it, you will remember my words.[55]

This stern warning got the desired results.

The next day (perhaps September 20), Xerxes ordered his warships, numbering almost 600, into the narrow Salamis strait. He climbed a nearby hill to watch the conflict, at first confident that the fewer than 350 vessels in the combined Greek fleets would have no chance against his forces. To his mounting horror, however, the Greek ships steadily hemmed in the Persian galleys on one side of the strait. Just as Themistocles had foreseen, the greater Persian numbers proved a disadvantage in the confined space, as those Persian ships moving forward got in the way of those retreating. As later captured by the Athenian playwright Aeschylus, who fought in the battle, Greek sailors and hoplites then moved in and slaughtered the terrified enemy by the thousands. In his play, *The Persians*, a messenger tells Xerxes' mother:

At once ship into ship battered its brazen beak. A Greek ship charged first, and chopped off the whole stern of a Persian galley. Then charge followed charge on every side. At first by its huge impetus our fleet withstood them. But soon, in that narrow space, our ships were jammed in hundreds; none could help another. They rammed each other with their prows of bronze; and some were stripped of every oar. Meanwhile the enemy came round us in a ring and charged. Our vessels heeled over; the sea was hidden, carpeted with wrecks and dead men; all the shores and reefs were full of dead. Then every ship we had broke rank and rowed for life. The Greeks seized fragments of wrecks and broken oars and hacked and stabbed at our men swimming in the sea. . . . The whole sea was one din of shrieks and dying groans, till night and darkness hid the scene.[56]

Maintaining Security Against a New Enemy

The Greeks followed up this win with others the following year (479 B.C.), including a tremendous victory over the Persian land army at Plataea, north of Athens. Even with the Persian menace removed, however, Themistocles saw that Athens must not lower its guard; in the coming years it would surely have to deal with an enemy closer to home, namely Sparta. With this in mind, he immediately and boldly acted to ensure Athenian security against possible Spartan aggression. The Persians had wrecked most of Athens's defensive walls. And the Spartans, as well as other Greeks worried about the rapid ongoing rise of Athenian power, did not want them rebuilt.

"The fact was," writes Themistocles' Roman biographer Cornelius Nepos,

> that the Athenians by their two victories at Marathon and Salamis had gained such prestige all over Greece that the Spartans knew that it was with them that they must contend for the hegemony [supremacy in Greece]. Therefore they wished the Athenians to be as weak as possible, and as soon as they learned that the walls were rising, they sent envoys to Athens to put a stop to the work.[57]

Themistocles then proceeded to trick the Spartans. He sent the envoys back to Sparta and soon afterward traveled there himself on the pretext of discussing the matter further. While he stalled for time, back in Athens every able-bodied person labored, at his prearranged orders, to restore the walls. In this and other ways, he strengthened Athens, leaving it free to build its naval empire.

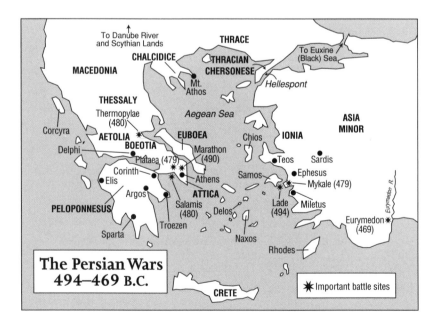

The Persian Wars
494–469 B.C.

✴ Important battle sites

Political Decline and Death

In the 470s B.C., however, even as Athens's empire began to take shape, Themistocles steadily lost political ground to younger leaders, chief among them Cimon, son of Miltiades. While Themistocles' policies remained firmly anti-Spartan, Cimon and his supporters thought it best to work with, rather than against, the Spartans; and circa 471, they managed to get Themistocles ostracized. At first he went to the Peloponnesus, where he continued to voice his anti-Spartan sentiments. Hoping to silence him, the Spartans eventually claimed they had proof he was collaborating with the Persian king, a charge that is almost certainly false. Unfortunately for Themistocles many of his countrymen believed the charges and the Athenian state accused him of treason, forcing him to flee from one part of Greece to another.

Cimon, one of Themistocles' political opponents in the 470s B.C., who became known for his pro-Spartan policies.

About 467, having run out of friendly refuges, Themistocles turned, probably very reluctantly, to the very foreigner he had been accused of helping—the Persian monarch (Artaxerxes, Xerxes' son). All of the ancient sources agree that Artaxerxes appointed the former Athenian archon and admiral as governor of the Persian city of Magnesia, in Asia Minor. There Themistocles died about 463 near the age of sixty. According to Thucydides:

> His bones, it is said, were conveyed home by his relatives in accordance with his wishes, and interred in Attic ground. This was done without the knowledge of the Athenians, as it was against the law to bury in Attica an outlaw for treason.[58]

The victor of Salamis was gone; yet his spirit remained. His enemies' triumph over him was brief, for in time his advocacy of naval power and misgivings about Sparta proved sound judgments. And when Athens attained its full flower of greatness under Pericles, many saw that it had done so, as Podlecki says, "only because Themistocles had planted the seeds."[59]

CHAPTER 4

Pericles: Athens's Guide to Its Greatest Age

The name Pericles has come to be synonymous with the so-called golden age of ancient Athens, the period lasting from the end of the Greco-Persian wars in 479 B.C. to the outbreak of the Peloponnesian conflict in 431. Later Greeks came to call it, often nostalgically, the *Pentakontaetia,* or "Fifty Years." In this short span, one or two generations of Athenian artists, sculptors, playwrights, and democratic reformers created a cultural legacy that still influences and awes Western society. "Future ages will wonder at us," Pericles himself correctly predicted, "as the present age wonders at us now." [60]

The southwest corner of the Parthenon, symbol of the Athenian golden age that Pericles helped to create.

Ironically, however, while it generated a great deal of *con*structive endeavor, the Fifty Years also laid the groundwork for Greece's most *de*structive period. These years saw ever-worsening relations between Athens and Sparta and their respective federations of allies. More than a generation of ill feeling and on-and-off fighting finally led to the devastating Peloponnesian War, which channeled Athenian energies into less creative avenues.

Pericles, the most dynamic, talented, and popular statesman-general of the age, was in large degree Athens's guiding force in these years. "Great as Athens had been when he became her leader," declares Plutarch, "he made her the greatest and richest of all cities." [61] To achieve a realistic and balanced view of Pericles' accomplishments, however, we must recognize that his often belligerent attitude toward other Greek states, especially Sparta, was a major cause of the great war. On the one hand he was an enlightened democrat and intellectual who encouraged artists and erected grand public buildings. On the other, he was an ardent imperialist who sought to expand Athenian power at the expense of its neighbors, frequently by means of threats, bribery, and when necessary naked military force.

It is reasonable to ask how Pericles managed to wield such influence, whether for good or ill. He was, after all, neither a president nor a prime minister, and in fact possessed no more political authority than a number of other Athenians; yet as Plutarch remarks, "he came to hold more power in his hands than many a king and tyrant." [62] His distinguished modern biographer, Donald Kagan, elaborates and offers an explanation:

Ancient depictions of Pericles, like this famous bust, almost always showed him wearing a helmet.

> Pericles . . . possessed no great private fortune. The citizen of a democratic republic, he held no office higher than that of general (*strategos*), one of ten, none of whom had greater formal powers than any of the others. He controlled no military or police forces, and he could expend no public money without a vote of the popular assembly of citizens. . . . Each year he had to stand for reelection and was constantly subject to public scrutiny and political challenge. . . . [The influence that] Pericles [possessed derived from] . . . the power of his ideas, the strength of his personality, the use of reason, and his genius as a uniquely persuasive rhetorician [public speaker]. In ancient Athens, the people decided policy in oral debate in the open air. Skill in public speaking was essential, and Pericles was the greatest orator of his day by common consent.[63]

Avoiding the Limelight

Pericles was born about 495 B.C. His father, the respected politician-general Xanthippus (pronounced zan-THIP-us), helped to prosecute Miltiades in 489 but then himself suffered ostracism five

The ruins of the Theater of Dionysus, where plays like Aeschylus's The
Persians, *which Pericles sponsored, were presented.*

years later. During the second Persian invasion, however, the people recalled Xanthippus from exile and he went on to defeat the Persians in a battle fought in Asia Minor. Pericles' mother, Agariste, was a niece of the democratic reformer Cleisthenes, of the Alcmeonid clan.

Not much of a definite nature is known about Pericles' early years. According to Plutarch, as a young man he kept a low profile, tending "to shrink from facing the people." [64] One reason for this, Plutarch claims, is that Pericles bore a striking resemblance to the former tyrant Pisistratus and wanted to avoid remarks to that effect. Plutarch also records that Pericles' head

> was rather long and out of proportion. For this reason almost all his portraits show him wearing a helmet, since the artists apparently did not wish to taunt him with this deformity. However, the comic poets of Athens nicknamed him "*schinocephalus*," or "squill-head." [65]

Plutarch says that another reason Pericles stayed out of politics at first was the rash of ostracisms in the 480s and 470s. His own father, as well as the politician Themistocles, had been banished, and he feared he might suffer the same fate. Whatever his reasons for avoiding the limelight, Pericles evidently remained content to serve as an ordinary soldier until he was in his midtwenties.

Political Heir to Themistocles

Eventually, Pericles did make his way into public life. However, his first known public role, as the *choregus* (sponsor) of a play, still allowed him to remain largely in the background. The year was 472 B.C. and the play was *The Persians*, by Aeschylus, the greatest dramatist of the day. At the time, the play was politically controversial because it promoted the importance of the Battle of Salamis, and by inference, the man who had engineered the victory—Themistocles. At the time, Themistocles was being assailed by conservative politicians; and in presenting the play, both Aeschylus and Pericles revealed their sympathy for Themistocles' liberal policies.

In fact, in the years after Themistocles' ostracism, Pericles steadily emerged as his political heir. For a while, Pericles functioned as chief assistant to Ephialtes, leader of the more liberal politicians. They opposed the pro-Spartan, pro-aristocratic, and generally old-fashioned politics of the conservatives, led by the popular statesman-general Cimon. In 463, Pericles attempted to get rid of Cimon by prosecuting him for bribery; but he was unable to get a conviction.

The following year, however, Ephialtes introduced a bill calling for a radical reduction in the powers of the conservative Areopagus, which strongly supported Cimon. The bill passed and the democrats, according to Aristotle, "stripped [the Areopagus] of its added powers . . . and assigned some of them to the [Council of] Five Hundred, and others to the people [i.e., the Assembly] and to the jury-courts." [66] After this reform, the main authority left to the Areopagus was that of hearing murder cases.

Two more crucial incidents then took place in rapid succession. Cimon fell out of favor with the people and was ostracized; and Ephialtes was assassinated, probably by some disgruntled conservatives.[67] The sum effect of all these events was that in 461 Pericles suddenly found himself the most popular leader in Athens. No one, including himself, could have guessed at that moment that he would remain at the pinnacle of state power for over thirty years.

Strengthening Democracy

A new and ultimately the greatest phase of the Fifty Years began with Pericles' rise to power. Technically, he was but one of the ten annually elected *strategoi*, who commanded the army and carried out the people's foreign policies. And initially, he was not the most experienced and influential *strategos*. Older generals, among them Myronides, Leocrates, and Tolmides, each probably held more individual authority in the Assembly. But likely because of Pericles' youth, energy, popularity, and extraordinary talent for oratory, his nine colleagues often deferred to his judgment or allowed him to speak for them. During the turbulent decades that followed, he managed to retain his high position by repeatedly winning reelection as general.

One of the first bills Pericles pushed through the Assembly on his own ended up both initiating a long series of Athenian democratic reforms and heating up the growing rivalry between Athens and Sparta. It was clear to Pericles and his supporters that the city walls Themistocles had built in the early 470s B.C. were inadequate to stop a Spartan invasion, since the enemy could simply camp outside the walls and starve the Athenians into submission. Landlocked Athens needed a way to tap into its naval lifeline at Piraeus. Pericles convinced the people to construct the Long Walls, a defensive perimeter stretching all the way to Piraeus. This safe-access corridor to the sea permitted a virtually unlimited flow of food and other supplies, transforming Athens, in Donald Kagan's words, "into an island unassailable by land and invincible so long as it retained command of the sea." [68]

The completion of the Long Walls, circa 457, did more than make Athens a formidable fortress. The many lower-class laborers and sailors who lived and worked in the port area now felt more connected to the urban center and began playing a bigger role in city politics. This increased participation by ordinary citizens

This modern map of fifth-century B.C. Athens and Piraeus shows the Long Walls, proposed by Pericles, stretching between.

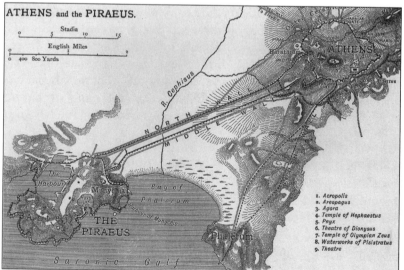

made the Assembly more democratic and responsive to the people's needs. Other democratic reforms followed. Pericles pushed through a bill providing pay for jurors, allowing poor people, who before could not afford to take time away from work to serve the state, to do so. He also eliminated rules stipulating that only those who met certain financial qualifications could hold high office. "The central fact of Periclean Athens," comments historian Charles A. Robinson, "was full participation of its citizens in the government of city and empire." [69]

The so-called Porch of the Maidens, on the south side of the Erechtheum, an integral part of Pericles' Acropolis complex.

Creative Self-Expression and Visual Propaganda

If open democracy was the central fact of Periclean Athens, its central achievement was its magnificent creative outburst. And the most visible aspect of this activity was the massive building program that climaxed in the 440s and 430s B.C. with the erection of the Parthenon and other temples on the Acropolis. Pericles told his countrymen that it was time for Athens to realize its enormous potential; it must show the world that it was invincible and eternal, that the gods had chosen it above all other states. "You must yourselves realize the power of Athens," he said (according to Thucydides),

> and feast your eyes upon her from day to day, till love of her fills your hearts; and then when all her greatness shall break upon you, you must reflect that it was by courage, sense of duty, and a keen feeling of honor in action that men were enabled to win all this. [70]

What better way to demonstrate that Athens was the marvel of Greece, Pericles asked, than by celebrating and honoring the goddess whose divine guidance was instrumental in the city's rise to greatness? Building new, grand, and beautiful temples to Athena would ensure her continued protection, he proposed. At the same time, a new and magnificent Acropolis complex would be the ultimate symbol of Athenian imperial greatness. "The sculptures of

51

This magnificent painting, by nineteenth-century artist Lawrence Alma-Tadema, shows Pericles and others watching Phidias at work on the Parthenon.

the Parthenon," says noted scholar Peter Green, "were to provide visual propaganda, in the broadest sense of the term." [71] And they fulfilled this purpose far beyond their builders' dreams. As Plutarch wrote centuries later:

> There was one measure above all which at once gave the greatest pleasure to the Athenians, adorned their city and created amazement among the rest of mankind, and which is today the sole testimony that the tales of the ancient power and glory of Greece are no mere fables. By this I mean his construction of temples and public buildings. [72]

Yet while Pericles provided the inspiration for the grand new project, it was the combined effort of hundreds of talented builders, sculptors, and artists who made it a reality. Encouraged and lavishly funded by the state, their energies and creativity suddenly received an outlet; and they took full advantage of the opportunity. Greek historian John Miliadis writes:

> It was not merely the passion for building . . . nor was it merely an exhibition of power. It was something deeper than all this. It was the irrepressible need of a whole generation which took the highest intellectual view of life, to find a creative self-expression. [73]

Trying to Do Too Much Too Fast

The drive for self-expression and personal distinction that motivated Athens's artists propelled its politicians as well. And this proved its undoing in the long run. For beginning in the early 450s B.C., enacting policies initiated by Pericles and his supporters, Athens involved itself in numerous political and military conflicts, both local and foreign; and it inevitably overextended itself, wasting many of its resources in an attempt to achieve too much too fast. "Driven by an amazing energy," writes classical scholar Peter Levi, the Athenians

> were asserting a supremacy that no one city could sustain, and even though the sea was theirs, with its commerce, the mines and the green riches of the earth, they could no more finally dominate the eastern Mediterranean than the Spartans could.[74]

One of the most glaring examples of the Athenians' taking on too much and suffering for it was their ill-fated Egyptian expedition. In the early 450s, Athens sent a large number of ships and soldiers to help the Egyptians in their rebellion against the Persians (who had conquered Egypt about seventy years before). At first, all went well, but in 456 the Persians launched a massive counterattack; in 454 almost the entire Athenian force was wiped out.[75] "This was a disaster of the greatest magnitude for Athens," says Kagan.

> Its psychological impact must have been even more damaging than the loss of men and ships. It broke an uninterrupted series of Athenian victories over Persia [and] caused serious unrest in the Aegean.[76]

The disaster did not dissuade Pericles and other Athenian leaders from continuing their forceful foreign policy, however. In the years that followed, they transformed the Delian League, the alliance of Greek states that had been created in the early 470s to safeguard Greece from Persia, into an empire of Athenian subject states. It was Pericles who transferred the League's funds from the Aegean island of Delos to Athens and later sanctioned their use to fund Athenian building programs. Many Greeks called this transfer outright theft.

It was also Pericles who in 440 led an expedition against the island of Samos, which had dared to rebel against Athenian rule. The Samians held out for nine months but finally had to surrender. Most Greeks, apparently including a number of Athenians, thought this episode shameful. Plutarch captured their feelings in a vignette in which Cimon's sister tells Pericles: "You have thrown away the lives of these brave citizens of ours, not in a war against the Persians . . . such as my brother Cimon fought, but in destroying a Greek city which is one of our allies."[77]

Meanwhile, many other Athenian soldiers died fighting the Spartans. Sparta had long been suspicious of Athenian democracy and expansionist policies, both of which it viewed as dangerous to the political and military stability of the Greek world. Suspicion turned to alarm in 459, as Athens drew the city-state of Megara away from Sparta's Peloponnesian alliance and began building in Megarian territory a defensive wall, designed to keep the Spartans from marching on Athens. Pericles' construction of the Athenian Long Walls soon afterward, expressly against Sparta's wishes, added insult to injury. In 457, the Spartans and Athenians, each reinforced by various allies, clashed at Tanagra, about twenty miles east of Thebes. The immediate outcome was indecisive. But the battle foreshadowed more and worse Athenian-Spartan conflicts to come.

Efforts to Discredit Him

Tensions and wars with neighbors were not the only challenges Pericles faced. Although his overall popularity in Athens long remained high, he still had his political enemies, who tried their best to discredit him. Among other things, they accused him of stealing the Delian League's treasury, of associating with "suspicious" intellectuals and foreigners, and of holding uncommon religious views.

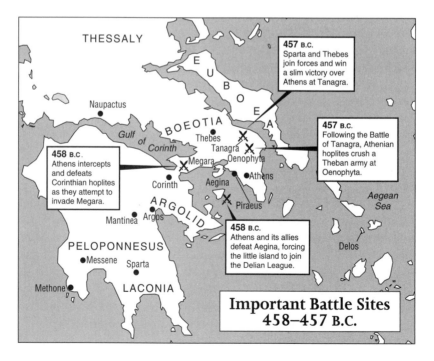

457 B.C.
Sparta and Thebes join forces and win a slim victory over Athens at Tanagra.

457 B.C.
Following the Battle of Tanagra, Athenian hoplites crush a Theban army at Oenophyta.

458 B.C.
Athens intercepts and defeats Corinthian hoplites as they attempt to invade Megara.

458 B.C.
Athens and its allies defeat Aegina, forcing the little island to join the Delian League.

Important Battle Sites 458–457 B.C.

When such attacks repeatedly had little effect, Pericles' opponents eventually went after his friends. In the 430s B.C., his old teacher, Anaxagoras the philosopher, went into exile rather than face an upcoming charge of impiety (showing irreverence toward the gods). Another of Pericles' associates, Phidias the sculptor, and Pericles' mistress (or common-law wife), Aspasia, with whom he lived for some twenty years, were actually tried for impiety.[78] Phidias was found guilty and went into exile; Aspasia was acquitted after Pericles himself made an impassioned speech on her behalf in court. (Aspasia may also have been targeted because she was a highly educated, confident, and outspoken woman in a society that expected women to be quiet and submissive.)

Pericles' friend Phidias, later acknowledged as the greatest sculptor of the ancient world, was tried and forced into exile.

War and Disillusionment

None of these indirect attempts to discredit Pericles worked, however. When he did finally lose favor with many Athenians, it was not because of any alleged corruption or improprieties, but rather because of his willingness to go to war rather than back down from his policy of expansion. In 435, a civil war erupted on the island of Corcyra, a Corinthian colony located off Greece's northwestern coast. Pericles involved Athens in the conflict in 433, supposedly to aid beleaguered Corcyrean democrats. As tensions mounted, Corinth appealed to Sparta to intervene against Athens, but the Spartans held off.

Rather than do the same, which would have been the more prudent course, Pericles decided that another show of Athenian force was in order. He imposed a trade embargo on Megara, which had recently switched its allegiance back to Sparta. Months went by, and as the Megarians began to starve, the threat of full-scale war loomed large. Many Greeks, a growing number of Athenians among them, urged Pericles to call off the blockade. According to Plutarch:

> It seems likely that the Athenians might have avoided war
> . . . if only they could have been persuaded to lift their embargo against the Megarians and come to terms with

them. And since it was Pericles who opposed this solution more strongly than anyone else . . . it was he alone that was held responsible for the war.[79]

After the commencement of the terrible Peloponnesian War in 431, many Athenians were equally disillusioned with Pericles' overall strategy. His plan was to allow the Spartans and their allies to invade Attica and pillage Athenian farms and villages. Meanwhile, the Athenians would hide behind the Long Walls. There, he said, the people would be safe and well supplied by cargo ships, while Athens took advantage of its control of the sea by attacking the coasts of the Peloponnesus. "We must not cry over the loss of houses and land," Pericles told his distraught countrymen,

> but of men's lives; since houses and land do not gain men, but men them. And if I thought that I could persuade you, I would have bid you go out and lay them waste with your own hands, and show the Peloponnesians that this at any rate will not make you submit.[80]

At first, Pericles' strategy seemed to work. But the plan had not anticipated an attack by an enemy ultimately more deadly than the Spartans. In 429 a plague (which remains unidentified) struck Athens, a pestilence that wiped out a fifth or more of the city's population. Later that year Pericles himself contracted the disease and died at about the age of sixty-six.

It is uncertain whether at that moment the Athenians understood the true significance of this loss. Pericles had been arrogant, stubborn, often impetuous, and sometimes unfeeling and brutal, to be sure. But he had also been an inspiring, just, inventive, endlessly energetic, and unswervingly patriotic leader. This unique mix of qualities had made him precisely the right person at the right time to guide his countrymen to greatness. That he also condemned them to destruction by embroiling them in the great war is perhaps an unfair charge. For had he survived the plague, he might have led them to victory or secured a lasting peace. What is certain is that, despite his faults, Athens never again produced a leader of his caliber.

CHAPTER 5

Alcibiades:
Beloved Rogue and
Infamous Traitor

"He was a man of many strong passions, but none of them was stronger than the desire to challenge others and gain the upper hand over his rivals."[81] This is how Plutarch summed up the character of Alcibiades, one of the most flamboyant, talented, and loved, but also inconsistent, untrustworthy, and hated figures in Greek history. On the one hand, he was handsome and engaging, a persuasive public speaker, a brilliant diplomat, and a highly capable soldier and general; on the other, he was arrogant in the extreme, prone to excessive drinking, sexual escapades, and other private pleasures, consumed by a desire for personal glory, and an incurable liar, con man, and traitor to his country. Of this truly larger-than-life character, his Roman biographer Cornelius Nepos wrote: "All men marveled that one man could have so varied and contradictory a character."[82]

Alcibiades emerged as an important Athenian leader at the height of the destructive Peloponnesian War. Elected as *strategos* on numerous occasions, he frequently swayed the Assembly to back his policies and several times led his countrymen to victory over Sparta and its allies. But his foreign policy, which was most often based on self-promotion, was unwise. He involved Athens in a large-scale military venture that ended in the most catastrophic defeat in the city's long history. And this, along with his other serious errors in judgment, proved a major factor in Athens's ultimate defeat in the war. As Thucydides put it, though Alcibiades' talent and potential were enormous, his unstable nature ultimately alienated his countrymen, and this "caused them to commit affairs [of state] to other [and less capable] hands, and thus before long to ruin the city."[83]

A Rowdy and Reckless Youth

Born about 450 B.C. into a well-to-do Athenian family, Alcibiades enjoyed a privileged childhood. His mother, Deinomache, was a member of the prestigious Alcmeonid clan, making him a close kinsman of Pericles, the foremost statesman of the day. When Alcibiades' father, Cleinias, was killed in battle in 447, Pericles took the boy in and reared him.

It soon became obvious to all that Alcibiades was an uncommon individual, both physically and mentally. "As for his physical beauty," Plutarch tells us,

> we need say no more than that it flowered at each season of his growth in turn, and lent him an extraordinary grace and charm, alike as a boy, a youth, and a man. [The great Athenian playwright] Euripides' saying that even the autumn of beauty possesses a loveliness of its own is not universally true. But if it applies to few others, it was certainly true of Alcibiades on account of his natural gifts and his physical perfection. Even his lisp is said to have suited his voice well and to have made his talk persuasive and full of charm.[84]

Plutarch and other ancient writers passed on various stories about Alcibiades' willful, spoiled, crafty, and self-indulgent behavior in childhood. Many of these were probably manufactured later; but some may be true or almost so, since Alcibiades often displayed these same kinds of behavior after he grew up. Describing his vanity and reckless behavior as a young man, Plutarch said that he

> lived a life of prodigious luxury, drunkenness, debauchery [sexual excess], and insolence. He was effeminate [womanly] in his dress and would walk through the marketplace trailing his long purple robes, and he spent extravagantly. He had the decks of his triremes [ships] cut away to allow him to sleep more comfortably, and his bedding was slung on cords, rather than spread on the hard planks. He had a golden shield made for him, which was emblazoned not with any ancestral device [decoration, as was the usual custom] but with the figure of Eros [god of love] armed with a thunderbolt. The leading men of Athens watched all this with disgust and indignation.[85]

Other Athenians evidently thought Alcibiades' rowdy youthful behavior glamorous, or refreshingly different, or at least harmless. And in fact several older men sought his friendship. One of these was the philosopher Socrates, about twenty years his senior.

Socrates tried to cultivate and encourage the many good qualities Alcibiades possessed, and the arrogant youth apparently respected this sometimes mentor more than any other person. It was said that the two were so close that they shared a tent when fighting together as soldiers in 432 and that Socrates saved the life of his eighteen-year-old friend. "There was a fierce battle," Plutarch wrote,

> in which they both fought with great courage, but when Alcibiades was wounded and fell, it was Socrates who stood over his body and defended him with the most conspicuous bravery and saved his life and his arms [weapons and armor] from the enemy.[86]

War and Peace, and War

Alcibiades first began playing a major role in Athenian politics circa 420 B.C., when he was about thirty. At that time he was first elected to the board of ten generals. Though an aristocrat, he was an advocate of radical democracy, as Themistocles and Pericles had been; also like them, he was strongly anti-Spartan. This prompted him to urge his countrymen to take a belligerent stance toward Sparta at a time when peace seemed on the horizon.

The great war had been raging for over a decade. After Pericles died in 429, two factions had fought to control Athenian foreign

This nineteenth-century painting renders a highly romanticized vision of Socrates tutoring the later infamous Alcibiades.

policy. One, led by a left-wing politician named Cleon, wanted to keep fighting until Athens had gained a clear victory. The other party, headed by the more conservative and cautious Nicias, favored making peace with Sparta. For several years the Assembly had backed Cleon's more aggressive policy and bloody fighting between the two opposing blocs of poleis had continued. In 422, however, both Cleon and Sparta's ablest general, Brasidas, had died in battle. Nicias had then managed to win over the Assembly. After he had made peace overtures to Sparta, the following year the combatants, weary of war, had signed a treaty known as the Peace of Nicias.

But the new peace turned out to be short-lived, in part because some of Sparta's allies, most prominently Corinth and Thebes, passionately hated Athens and wanted no peace until they had crushed it. But the main reason the peace failed was that Alcibiades hated Sparta with equal passion and promoted moves that triggered new hostilities. In 420 he persuaded his countrymen to make an alliance with Sparta's enemy, Argos, as well as with two other Peloponnesian cities, Mantinea and Elis. Realizing that Sparta would see this alliance as an act of war, Nicias tried to stop it, but to no avail. The immediate result, just as Alcibiades had expected, was a resumption of the war. But subsequent events did not favor Athens, as he had hoped, for in a major battle fought near Mantinea in 418, the Spartans decisively defeated Athens, Argos, and their allies.[87]

The Syracusan Expedition

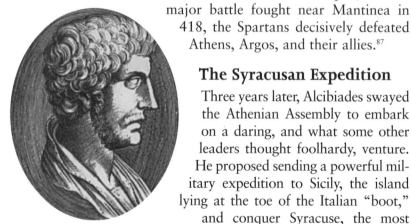

This portrait of Alcibiades, created long after his death, attempts to portray him as a troubled individual.

Three years later, Alcibiades swayed the Athenian Assembly to embark on a daring, and what some other leaders thought foolhardy, venture. He proposed sending a powerful military expedition to Sicily, the island lying at the toe of the Italian "boot," and conquer Syracuse, the most splendid of the Greek cities in that region. Defeating Syracuse, he argued, would give Athens control of Sicily's considerable wealth, foodstuffs, and soldiers, and with it a decisive edge over Sparta and its allies. Once more, it was Nicias who opposed Alcibiades and urged caution. "From all that I hear," Nicias warned, we are going against cities that are great and not . . . in the least likely to accept our rule in exchange for freedom. . . . These [cities] are full of hoplites, archers, and dart-throwers, have triremes [warships] in abundance and multitudes to man them.[88]

But Alcibiades discounted Nicias's testimony:

The cities in Sicily are peopled by motley rabbles. . . . The inhabitants, being without any feeling of patriotism, are not provided with arms for their persons. . . . Moreover, the Sicilians have not so many hoplites as they boast . . . [and] we shall have the help of many barbarians [non-Greeks], who from their hatred of the Syracusans will join us in attacking them. . . . Be convinced then that we shall augment [increase] our power at home by this adventure abroad, and let us make the expedition, and so humble the pride of the Peloponnesians. . . . Do not let the passive policy which Nicias advocates . . . turn you from your purpose.[89]

To the regret of Nicias and others who did not trust Alcibiades, a majority in the Assembly approved the plan. And as Thucydides says, "The few who did not like it feared to appear unpatriotic by holding up their hands [i.e., voting] against it, and so kept quiet."[90] In hopes of fostering unity, the people placed Nicias in joint command of the expedition, along with Alcibiades. Over 130 ships, carrying some 5,000 hoplites and thousands of light-armed troops and sailors, sailed for Sicily.

The vessels had no sooner reached that island than an Athenian galley arrived to take Alcibiades back for trial. Shortly before the expedition's departure, some unknown culprits had defaced several statues of the god Hermes and Alcibiades' enemies had accused him of masterminding the crime.[91] Unwilling to risk conviction, on the way back to Athens he escaped. Turning his back on his country, he fled to the last place anyone would have expected him to go—Sparta, which gave him refuge. On hearing of this treachery, his shocked countrymen condemned him to death and confiscated his property.

Traitorous Activities

Alcibiades' flight left Nicias, a far less talented commander, in charge of the Syracusan expedition. His heart not in the venture, Nicias blockaded the city's harbor but was slow to mount a full-scale attack. While he delayed, Alcibiades convinced the Spartans

The Athenian fleet assembles in Syracuse's harbor. The expedition ended in failure in large degree because Alcibiades abandoned it.

that they might deal Athens a death blow by sending a strong force of hoplites to aid the Syracusans. The Spartans took this advice; despite the arrival of Athenian reinforcements, in 413 a combined force of Spartans and Syracusans completely defeated the Athenians. Nicias and his fellow commanders were executed and most of the seven thousand Athenians who survived the slaughter ended up in a living hell as slaves in Sicily's stone quarries. Thucydides called it the "total destruction" of "their fleet, their army," and "everything," and reported that "few out of many returned home." [92]

In 412, Alcibiades continued his traitorous activities by traveling around the eastern Aegean, attempting to stir up rebellions among Athens's allies in the area. He also appealed to Persia to enter the war as Sparta's ally. By the following year, however, he had abandoned the Spartans, who, rightly suspecting him of negotiating more in his own interest than theirs, no longer trusted him.

Hoping to return to Athens, in 411 Alcibiades became indirectly involved in a plot (partly backed by Persian gold that he had secured) that allowed a small group of antidemocratic Athenian politicians to displace the Assembly and rule in its stead. But the coup soon collapsed when the crews of the Athenian warships then stationed at Samos threatened to sail home and restore democracy by force. This turned out to be Alcibiades' big chance. Realizing that what they lacked most was competent leadership, the fickle Athenians recalled him from exile and made him a general once more.

A Man Without a Home

Though back in his countrymen's good graces, Alcibiades did not yet return to Athens. Keeping Samos as his base, he led naval forays against the Spartans, who had recently built their first major war fleet. The main theater of war had shifted to the western coast of Asia Minor, and especially the Hellespont and Propontis (the waterway lying between the Aegean and Black Seas), for the Spartans had made it their objective to cut off Athens's route to the supplies of grain it imported from Greek cities along the coasts of the Black Sea. Without these vital supplies, the Athenians could not sustain their large population for long. For four years, Alcibiades repeatedly thwarted Spartan attempts to gain control of these sea lanes. His most stunning victory occurred in 410 B.C. at Cyzicus, on the southern shore of the Propontis, where he sank or captured some sixty Spartan warships.

Having refurbished his image as Athens's "golden boy," in 407 Alcibiades made a triumphant return to the home he had not seen for eight years. His younger contemporary, Xenophon, later recorded the memorable scene:

> Dense crowds of people, not only from Piraeus but from Athens itself, gathered around the ships as he sailed in. Everyone wanted to see and to wonder at the sight of the great Alcibiades. . . . [He] brought his ship to anchor close to the shore. . . . When he caught sight of his cousin . . . and other relatives and friends, he landed from the ship and went up to Athens. . . . He then made speeches both in the Council and the Assembly in his own defense, stating that he had not been guilty of sacrilege and claiming that he had been unjustly treated. . . . Alcibiades was then proclaimed supreme commander with authority over all the other generals. He, it was thought, was the man who had the ability to reestablish the former power of Athens.[93]

Spartan and Syracusan hoplites inflict heavy casualties as they pursue the retreating Athenians across the Sicilian countryside near Syracuse.

But once again, Alcibiades did not live up to his countrymen's expectations. The following year he made the mistake of entrusting his fleet to a less-competent subordinate and a talented and aggressive Spartan commander named Lysander

As musicians play, the Spartans force the Athenians to tear down the Long Walls after Athens's surrender in 404 B.C.

soundly defeated it. The Athenians rightly blamed Alcibiades and voted him out of the office of *strategos*. Instead of returning home and enduring disgrace (and perhaps prosecution for negligence), he fled to a fortress on the shore of the Hellespont.

But he did not stay there for long. In 405, Lysander disastrously defeated the Athenians at Aegospotami, not far from Alcibiades' fortress, and closed off Athens's precious grain route. The Athenians surrendered the following year, and with the Spartans now in control of Greece, Alcibiades no longer felt safe. He took refuge with Pharnabazus, the governor of Persia's province in central Asia Minor. But the reality was that there were no safe places left for Athens's beloved rogue. At the request of Spartan leaders, Pharnabazus sent men to kill him.

"Alcibiades ended as he had lived," remarks historian Victor Ehrenberg, "as a great adventurer, a man without a home, a man without principles."[94] In the final analysis, this lack of principles, along with his arrogance and personal ambition, led him to make mistakes that negated his constructive deeds and kept him from fulfilling his great potential. Like Themistocles and Pericles, he dreamed large. But their dreams had been for Athens's glory; his were for his own. And the result was tragedy, both for him and his city.

CHAPTER 6

Epaminondas: Extraordinary Military Innovator and Strategist

Looking back on the long list of talented military leaders produced by ancient Greece, the name of Epaminondas looms large. The respected modern military historian Frank E. Adcock calls him "the greatest tactical innovator that the Greek city-states ever produced." [95] This opinion is hardly exaggerated; Epaminondas introduced dramatic improvements in the tactics of hoplite warfare that vaulted his native city of Thebes into its short but brilliant domination of Greece in the mid–fourth century B.C. Perhaps even more significantly, his innovations influenced the military organization of Philip II and his son Alexander, thus paving the way for the Macedonian rule later in the century.

Important as his military ideas and exploits were, Epaminondas was also renowned for his talent as a statesman and his exceedingly noble character. The first-century B.C. Greek historian Diodorus Siculus said of him:

Epaminondas, the talented Theban general who led his polis during its brief period of supremacy in Greece.

> He surpassed his contemporaries not only in skill and experience in the art of war, but in reasonableness and generosity as well. For among the generation of Epaminondas were famous men. . . . Still earlier than these. . . there were Solon, Themistocles, Miltiades, Cimon . . . and

Pericles. . . . If you should compare the qualities of these with the generalship and reputation of Epaminondas, you would find [his] qualities far superior. . . . For in strength of body and eloquence of speech . . . elevation of mind . . . fairness, and, most of all, in courage and shrewdness in the art of war, he far surpassed them all. So it was that in his lifetime his native country acquired the primacy of Greece, but when he died lost it.[96]

The Boeotian League

Not much is known about Epaminondas's life before his emergence as a leading Theban general in the late 370s B.C. He was probably born about 410, the year of Alcibiades' great naval victory at Cyzicus, in the final third of the disastrous Peloponnesian War. Cornelius Nepos claims that Epaminondas's father was Polymnis, an honorable Theban of modest means. The young man learned to play the lyre and to sing and dance, says Nepos, and excelled at wrestling and the use of arms. He also early displayed those qualities of character that made him famous as an adult—honesty, patience, courage, and a love of learning and culture.

During most of his youth, Epaminondas's native city, like most others in Greece, was dominated by Sparta, principal victor of the great war. Thebes did hold some modest local authority, in the small region of Boeotia (pronounced bee-OH-shya), where it had long been the recognized leader of the Boeotian League, a loose confederacy of about a dozen poleis. This tendency "towards Boeotian unification," writes Michael Grant,

> was a significant experiment in a type of inter-state union which generally eluded the Greeks of the classical period, with ultimate fatal results. But the new League could not—except perhaps theoretically—be regarded as an association of equals, since the Thebans, who became more prosperous and numerous after the Peloponnesian War, were always dominant.[97]

The Spartans feared the potential power of the Boeotian League enough to dissolve it about the year 386. But this situation was short-lived. In 382, some fifteen hundred Spartan hoplites occupied the Theban acropolis in support of a Spartan-backed coup against Thebes's democratic government, a move that amplified an already existing local hatred of Sparta. It also inspired patriotic resistance. In 379, Epaminondas's friend, the Theban leader Pelopidas, led a daring coup of his own, which overthrew the

Spartan-backed leaders and restored democracy.[98] Soon afterward, the Boeotian League was restored as well.

Standing Up to the Spartan Bully

Epaminondas was apparently already a leading Theban citizen at the time the Spartans were expelled. His activities in the following few years are obscure, but he had no doubt already gained the admirable reputation for wisdom that prompted one foreign dignitary to say that he had "never met anyone who knew more or spoke less."[99] What is certain is that by 371 B.C. Epaminondas's countrymen considered him important enough to make their leading envoy to a peace conference held that year in Sparta, a meeting attended by representatives from many of the war-weary Greek states. There, a serious dispute broke out between Epaminondas and one of Sparta's two kings, Agesilaus, who, like other Spartan leaders, still wanted to see the Boeotian League disbanded. According to Plutarch, Epaminondas

> delivered a speech not on behalf of his fellow Thebans but of Greece as a whole. In this he declared that war made the Spartans strong at the expense of all the other states, and insisted that peace should be founded upon terms of justice and equality. . . . Agesilaus . . . asked him whether he thought it just and equitable that the cities of Boeotia should be independent of Thebes. Epaminondas promptly and boldly responded with another question—did Agesilaus think it just and equitable that the cities of Laconia [the southern part of the Peloponnesus] should be independent of Sparta? [After the exchange escalated into an argument,] Agesilaus flew into a rage and [struck] the name of Thebes out of the peace treaty and [declared] war upon her.[100]

Soon afterward, the other Spartan king, Cleombrotus, led a formidable force of ten thousand hoplites toward Boeotia, bent on punishing Thebes and breaking up its confederacy.[101] Preparing to meet this threat, the Thebans made Epaminondas the leading *boeotarch* (Theban general). And as Diodorus reports, "having conscripted . . . all Thebans of military age and the other Boeotians who were willing and qualified, led forth from Thebes his army, numbering in all not more than six thousand."[102]

The Victory at Leuctra

Epaminondas and Pelopidas had been training the Theban troops for some time. Pelopidas had taken charge of the Sacred Band, a

The heavy-handed policies of Sparta's King Agesilaus, depicted here standing at left, helped to provoke the rise of Thebes.

unit of three hundred elite fighters, each of whom was a match for the best Spartan hoplite. Meanwhile, Epaminondas had drilled the main army in some new and unusual battlefield tactics. He had carefully observed the traditional way that Greek generals had arranged their infantry and noted that they placed their best troops on the right wing of the phalanx. When two opposing armies met, the strong right wings always faced weaker enemy left wings; the army with the most powerful right wing was usually able to crush the opposing left wing and then outflank, or move around and behind, the other army, assuring victory. As noted military historian Peter Connolly explains:

> Epaminondas believed that if he could knock out the crack Spartan troops on the right wing, the rest of the Spartan army would collapse. In order to achieve this, he planned

to reverse his battle order, placing his own weakest troops on the right, opposite the Spartan left, lining up the phalanx *en echelon* [obliquely, or at an angle], with the weakest troops held back, whilst at the same time massing his best troops on the left, supported by the strongest cavalry and the Sacred Band.[103]

To give his left wing even more power, Epaminondas made it fifty rows deep, compared with twelve rows of the Spartan right wing.[104]

The fateful battle that first tested these new tactics occurred in July 371 B.C., near Leuctra, a village ten miles southwest of Thebes. According to Diodorus:

> When the trumpets on both sides sounded the charge and the armies simultaneously with the first onset raised the battle cry . . . they met in hand-to-hand combat, [and] at first both fought ardently and the battle was evenly poised; shortly, however, as Epaminondas's men began to derive advantage from . . . the denseness of their lines, many Peloponnesians began to fall. For they were unable to endure the weight of the courageous fighting of the élite corps [the Sacred Band]. . . . The Spartans were with great difficulty forced back; at first, as they gave ground they would not break their formation, but finally, as many fell and the commander who would have rallied them [Cleombrotus] had died, the army turned and fled in utter rout.[105]

A modern sketch depicts the ruins on the site of ancient Thebes, which under Epaminondas achieved much power and prestige.

The plan had succeeded with brutal efficiency. A thousand Spartans, including their king, had been slain; while the Boeotians had lost just forty-seven men. In this single stroke, Epaminondas had dispelled the myth of Spartan invincibility and paved the way for a Theban hegemony of Greece.

Police Actions in the Peloponnesus

The humbling of Sparta immediately changed the political climate of Greece, especially in the Peloponnesus. Supported by Thebes, most of the Peloponnesian cities that had long followed Sparta out of fear threw out their Spartan-backed oligarchies and proclaimed independence (most of them instituting some form of democracy). Many of the leading towns of Arcadia, the region encompassing the central Peloponnesus, formed a confederacy similar to the Boeotian League; and less than a year after the Battle of Leuctra, with Epaminondas's aid, they established a central capital, calling it Megalopolis ("great city").

A gorge in the Mt. Olympus range, in northern Thessaly, one of the Greek regions over which Thebes extended its influence.

Epaminondas next marched his army into Laconia and camped very close to Sparta (which had no defensive walls, since fear of the Spartan phalanx had always been enough to keep enemies away). It remains uncertain whether he intended to attack the city or merely to intimidate and humiliate the Spartans by showing them that he *could* do so if necessary. In any case, after a few weeks he withdrew his forces and entered Messenia, the region west of Sparta. The Spartans had long used outright brutality and terror to hold the Messenians in a state of virtual slavery (as serfs called helots), forcing them to work the fields and send most of what they produced to Sparta. Epaminondas liberated the region from Spartan domination and helped the Messenians found a new fortified city of their own, Messene. As he had expected, the loss of Messenia was a devastating blow to Sparta, which had heavily relied on the grain it had imported from the region.

In the following few years, Epaminondas marched his troops into the Peloponnesus three more times. He and his fellow Theban leaders discovered to their dismay that, despite their usually good intentions, it was impossible to maintain political balance and stability in Greece without periodically resorting to force and/or alienating one state or another. Athens remained hostile to the Theban hegemony; unrest in Thessaly, north of Boeotia, required armed Theban intervention on more than one occasion; and relations between Thebes and the Arcadian confederacy (as well as among the confederacy's own members) became increasingly strained.

Epaminondas's Daughters

The last police action Epaminondas felt compelled to take in the Peloponnesus occurred in 362 B.C. Open warfare had recently broken out between some of the Arcadian cities and the nearby city-state of Elis (which hosted the Olympic games every four years). Tensions among the central Peloponnesian states had subsequently grown, Sparta had become involved, and the Thebans had found it impossible to resolve the situation without resorting to force.

Reaching Mantinea (north of Megalopolis) in late summer, Epaminondas's army faced a powerful coalition of hoplites from Sparta, Athens, Elis, and various Arcadian cities. The battle that ensued was the largest ever fought by Greeks against Greeks up to that time, involving over fifty thousand combatants in all.[106] Epaminondas aligned his forces in an oblique formation, as he had at Leuctra, and once more gained an advantage, although this time it was not as decisive, since his opponents had anticipated his tactics. The battle ended more or less in a draw. According to Xenophon, "Both sides claimed the victory, but it cannot be said that with regard to the accession of new territory, or cities, or power either side was any better off after the battle than before it."[107]

Yet the outcome of the struggle at Mantinea was still momentous, for Epaminondas had fallen in the fighting. Diodorus gives this account of his untimely end:

> When [the Spartans] saw that Epaminondas in the fury of battle was pressing forward too eagerly, they charged [at] him. . . . As the missiles flew thick and fast around him . . . he received a mortal wound in the chest. . . . About his body a rivalry ensued in which many were slain on both sides. . . . [Later, in his camp,] physicians were summoned, but . . . they declared that . . . as soon as the spear-point should be drawn from his chest, death would ensue. . . . [He asked] which side was victorious [and hearing it was his own] directed them to withdraw the spear-point. [One of his friends cried out] "You

71

Epaminondas lies mortally wounded after the Battle of Mantinea. Following his passing, Thebes lost its prominent place in Greek affairs.

die childless, Epaminondas," and burst into tears. To this he replied, "No, by Zeus, on the contrary, I leave behind two daughters, Leuctra and Mantinea, my victories." [108]

Having said this, he ordered that the spear-point be removed and died.

Epaminondas's countrymen had no leaders of his stature to replace him (Pelopidas having died in battle two years before), so Thebes was not able to maintain its dominance over Greek affairs. For the moment, the Greek cities, exhausted from years of strife, maintained an uneasy truce. They had no way of knowing that their days as independent states were numbered and that the man who would one day subjugate them would do so by using and further developing Epaminondas's military innovations.

CHAPTER 7

Philip: Political Opportunist and Unifier of Greece

In the autumn of 346 B.C., a Greek orator named Isocrates published an address calling for the Greek states to unite in a war against their old enemy, Persia. The Persians were cowards, Isocrates declared, and poor fighters. It would be more fitting for Persia's vast wealth to be in the hands of Greeks, who were inherently superior to Persians and other barbarians. Therefore, he concluded,

Philip II of Macedonia, who in an amazingly short period molded his kingdom's disorganized tribes into a mighty nation.

> I am now addressing myself to you although I am not unaware that when I am proposing this course many will look at it askance, but that when you are actually carrying it out all will rejoice in it. . . . I assert that it is incumbent on you to work for the good of the Greeks . . . and to extend your power over the greatest possible number of barbarians. For if you do . . . all men will be grateful to you.[109]

The "you" to whom Isocrates aimed his address was Philip II, king of Macedonia. At the time, Philip had just marched an army through the pass of Thermopylae and into southern Greece, shocking and alarming the citizens of Athens and other leading city-states. He was familiar with the aged orator and his long series of speeches urging an anti-Persian crusade. And it is likely that the Macedonian monarch had already seriously considered such a venture.

But Philip knew that no such Greek invasion of Persia would be practical until the city-states stopped fighting among themselves and united under a single strong leader. Isocrates and more than a few other Greeks had come to face the reality that Philip would be that leader. They had watched his rise from a young and inexperienced ruler of a kingdom on the fringes of the Greek world to a shrewd, capable master of a united nation with a powerful army. It seemed to Isocrates only a matter of time before Philip brought the disunited and war-weary Greek states under his domination.

And they were right. Philip went on to establish Macedonian domination of Greece and to begin preparations for the fateful invasion of Persia. Thus, Philip's policies and conquests set in motion a chain of events that, through his son's conquests, spread Greek culture throughout the Near East and ushered in what is now known as the Hellenistic Age. What Philip did above all, though, asserts Michael Grant,

> was to terminate the classical age of the autonomous city-states. . . . By and large their epoch [era] was ended. . . . Despite phenomenal successes in so many fields during the previous centuries, their mutually hostile fragmentation . . . had effectively destroyed any real possibility that they could form an effective union or federation of independent states by themselves. So Philip had to do it for them.[110]

The Sons of Amyntas

Philip was born about 382 B.C., the youngest son of Macedonia's King Amyntas III. At the time, the kingdom was divided, as it had been for centuries, between two distinct geographical and cultural regions. The kings usually held sway over the "lowlands," a small, fertile plain bordering the northwestern Aegean coast, while various local chieftains controlled the "highlands," a mountainous plateau partially encircling the plain. Attempts by earlier rulers to unite the kingdom had failed, as had several initiatives designed to move Macedonia into Greece's political and cultural mainstream. In the eyes of the city-state Greeks, Peter Green points out, Macedonia was a primitive and corrupt cultural backwater.

> They regarded Macedonians in general as semi-savages, uncouth of speech and dialect, retrograde in their political institutions, negligible as fighters, and habitual oath-breakers, who dressed in bear pelts and were much given to . . . [drunkenness], tempered with regular bouts of assassination and incest.[111]

Philip's first brush with the supposedly more civilized city-state Greeks came in 368, when he was about fourteen. His father, Amyntas, had recently died, leaving his eldest brother, Alexander II, on the throne. The new king proceeded to seize some towns in Thessaly, the region lying directly south of Macedonia. Trying to avert a destructive conflict, some Thessalian leaders requested that Thebes, then the dominant power in Greece, step in and settle the matter. The Theban general Pelopidas responded immediately. He created a buffer zone, guarded by Theban troops, between Thessaly and Macedonia. In the meantime, Alexander was murdered and Philip's other brother, Perdiccas III, became king. Pelopidas did not trust Perdiccas and his unstable royal court to keep the peace, so on returning home the Theban took with him a number of hostages, among them Philip.

For more than three years Philip resided in Thebes, where he was treated with the attention, kindness, and respect befitting his rank as an aristocrat. He stayed in the home of Pammenes, a *boeotarch* (general) and close associate of Epaminondas, then recognized as the leading military strategist in all of Greece. Exactly how much military science Philip learned directly from Epaminondas and other Theban generals is unclear.[112] But there is no doubt that Philip's later military tactics reflected Epaminondas's influence, even if indirectly.

During a furious battle, Epaminondas saves his friend Pelopidas's life. It was Pelopidas who brought young Philip as a hostage to Thebes.

A Powerful New Nation

In fact, perhaps a good deal sooner than he had expected, Philip found himself having to develop military tactics of his own. Late in 365 B.C., his brother, Perdiccas, arranged for his return to Macedonia and assigned him the difficult job of whipping the kingdom's small, largely ineffective army into fighting shape. Not long afterward Philip had to shoulder a far greater responsibility. In 359, Perdiccas was killed fighting the Illyrians, a hill people inhabiting the region northwest of Macedonia, leaving Philip, then about twenty-two or so, as Macedonia's new king.

At this juncture, Amyntas's last surviving son faced huge challenges that would surely have overwhelmed leaders of lesser talent, courage, and toughness. First, a number of local aristocrats refused to recognize his claim to the throne and several pretenders (would-be kings) challenged that claim. In addition, the Illyrians and another warlike mountain people, the Paeonians, prepared to invade Macedonia, which to all observers appeared to be coming apart at the seams. But none of Philip's domestic or foreign enemies had reckoned on the incredible political and military skills he possessed and now began to display. First, as a stopgap measure, he bribed the Illyrians and Paeonians to keep them from invading. He then spent the winter of 359–358 rigorously training and drilling whatever troops he could muster from the lowland clans. In the spring, he marched north and surprised the Paeonians, beating them in a small battle; and soon afterward, he attacked the far stronger Illyrians, gaining victory through the use of some of Epaminondas's tactics. As Peter Green tells it:

> Philip himself led the infantry, holding back his center and left, deploying his line in the oblique echelon that was Epaminondas's specialty. As he had anticipated, the Illyrian right wing stretched and slewed [twisted] round to force an engagement. Philip waited until the inevitable, fatal gap appeared [in the enemy's line] and then sent in his right-wing cavalry, flank and rear. They drove a great wedge through the gap, and the Macedonian phalanx followed in their wake. A long and desperate struggle ensued. But at last . . . 7,000 Illyrians . . . were slaughtered.[113]

Having secured Macedonia's northern frontiers, Philip proceeded with amazing speed to unify the country's lowlanders and highlanders into a single and powerful nation. His principal tool in this effort was the creation of Europe's first professional stand-

Pikemen of the lethal Macedonian phalanx, introduced by Philip, stand in close order in preparation for battle.

ing army. In sharp contrast to the militia utilized by the city-states, which were called up only when needed, Philip's army was a large permanent force whose members received extensive training. Philip also paid his soldiers handsome rewards, including parcels of land and the spoils gained in their victories. These incentives motivated thousands of young men from all over Macedonia to join Philip's new national organization.

The new military force that Philip developed consisted of several different elements, each of which supported and strengthened the others. One of these was an elite cavalry corps of young noblemen (first introduced by Philip's ancestor, Alexander I), known as the King's Companions (*hetairoi*). Long used mainly for skirmishing or guarding the king, the Companions were now trained to make frontal assaults on enemy lines. Philip also made the traditional Greek phalanx more formidable. First, he deepened its ranks, as Epaminondas had done; then he greatly increased the length of the soldiers' spears. These two-handed pikes (*sarissas*), ranging from twelve to eighteen feet long, projected from the front of the phalanx, forming an impenetrable, lethal mass of sharpened metal.[114] Though this "Macedonian phalanx," as it became known, was frighteningly effective, Philip made it even more so by supporting it with other offensive elements, including the Companion cavalry, archers, peltasts (javelin throwers), and innovative siege tactics.

"Fraud Before Force, but Force at the Least"

In the years that followed, Philip's new military system began to prove itself. In 357 B.C. he captured Amphipolis, a former Athenian colony located about seventy miles east of the Macedonian capital of Pella. Athens responded by declaring war, but this proved an empty gesture, since the Athenians were unwilling to send troops so far from home. Philip went on to seize the rich gold and silver mines located north of Amphipolis, from which he thereafter reaped an enormous annual income. (That same year, he married Olympias, princess of Epirus, a small kingdom lying southwest of Macedonia; and in 356 she bore him a son, Alexander III).

Philip was not satisfied only with Amphipolis, nor with Pydna, Potidaea, Methone, and the many other northern Aegean cities he captured in the next few years. He kept extending his influence southward, in the direction of Athens, Thebes, Corinth, and Greece's other major city-states, whose arts, architecture, and other aspects of high culture he greatly admired. It may well be that he already recognized that the small, independent polis was an outmoded concept and dreamed of forging the disunited city-states into one nation under a strong ruler, namely himself.

Whenever it was that Philip actually formulated this goal, naked force was not the only means he used to achieve it. Diodorus suggests that his success "was not due so much to his prowess in arms as to his adroitness and cordiality in diplomacy. Philip himself is said to have been prouder of his grasp of strategy and his diplomatic successes than of his valor in actual battle." [115] It must be emphasized, however, that Philip's negotiation techniques more often than not included intrigues, half-truths, and outright lies. The late noted scholar of Philip's career, David Hogarth, described his method of gaining territory as "fraud before force, but force at the least." [116] Another respected historian, J. F. C. Fuller, adds that Philip was

> an astute opportunist to whom success justified everything. He was recklessly brave, yet unlike so many brave generals he would at once set force aside should he consider that bribery or liberality or feigned friendship was more likely to secure his end. He possessed in marked degree the gift of divining what was in his enemy's mind and when beaten in the field would accept defeat and prepare for victory. [117]

In addition to his powerful army and political genius, another factor that greatly aided Philip's early successes was the failure of the major city-states to stop him, either singly or together. Indeed, for many years few important Greek public figures called attention to the threat he posed. The most influential of those who did was an Athenian—Demosthenes, the greatest orator Greece had ever produced. In 351, he delivered the first of his so-called Philippics, speeches denouncing Philip's aggressions. "Observe, Athenians, the height to which the fellow's insolence has soared," Demosthenes thundered:

> He leaves you no choice of action or inaction; he blusters and talks big . . . [and] he cannot rest content with what he has conquered; he is always taking in more, everywhere casting his net around us, while we sit idle and do nothing. When, Athenians, will you take the necessary action? What are you waiting for? Until you are compelled, I presume.[118]

Showdown at Chaeronea

Unfortunately for the Athenians and their neighbors, few of them heeded Demosthenes' words before it was too late to stop Philip. In 346 B.C., the year old Isocrates urged him to lead a united Greece against Persia, Philip entered southern Greece and took control of the religious sanctuary at Delphi, home of the famous oracle. At this point, says Plutarch, "The news stunned the Athenians. No speaker dared to mount the rostrum, nobody knew what advice should be given, the assembly was struck dumb and appeared to be completely at a loss."[119]

A major military showdown between Philip and the leading southern city-states now seemed inevitable (at least to those states, for evidence suggests that Philip would have been just as happy to become their master through diplomacy). Demosthenes became

A statue of Demosthenes, the great Athenian orator who repeatedly spoke out against Philip's aggressions.

The excavated remains of this small theater, in which one of Philip's subjects stabbed him to death, are located in the modern village of Vergina.

the man of the hour, almost single-handedly forging a powerful anti-Macedonian alliance headed by Athens and Thebes. In the summer of 338, Philip, accompanied by his son Alexander, now eighteen, marched his army (consisting of about thirty thousand infantry and two thousand cavalry) toward Thebes; the allies (with roughly thirty-five thousand infantry and two thousand cavalry) set up a defensive line in the Cephisus Valley near Chaeronea, in western Boeotia. The two forces clashed on August 4 in what proved to be one of the more decisive battles in Western history. Philip's victory was complete and the Greek city-states now faced the dawn of a new political order.

In the wake of Chaeronea, Philip treated some of the allies harshly, others rather leniently. In Thebes, he executed many leaders, confiscated their lands, and installed a military garrison on the city's acropolis, as Sparta had done years before. Then he broke up the Boeotian League. On the other hand, he treated the Athenians more mercifully, promising not to march his troops into Attica. In return, he demanded that Athens recognize him as head of the Greek confederacy he intended to create.[120]

That confederacy first came into being in September 338, when Philip presided over a grand assembly (*synedrion*) of many mainland and island poleis (the major absentee being Sparta, which remained stubbornly aloof). Peter Green summarizes the outcome:

The Greek states were to make a common peace . . . with one another, and constitute themselves into a federal Hellenic [Greek] League. This league would take joint decisions by means of a federal council . . . on which each state would be represented according to its size and military importance. . . . Simultaneously, the league was to form a separate alliance with Macedonia, though Macedonia itself would not be a member. This treaty was to be made with "Philip and his descendants" in perpetuity. The king would act as "leader" (hegemon) of the league's joint forces, a combined civil and military post designed to provide for the general security of Greece. . . . If the Greeks were involved in a war, they could call on Macedonia to support them. Equally, if Philip needed military aid, he was entitled to requisition contingents from the league.[121]

The Name of the King

Few Greeks were pleased with the new political arrangement Philip had imposed on them. But there was little or nothing they could do to stop him; and they now found themselves swept along in the tide of his plans for invading Persia. As it turned out, however, it was not Philip who ended up leading this fateful expedition, for in 336 B.C. a disgruntled Macedonian stabbed him to death at a wedding celebration. The Athenians and many other Greeks loudly celebrated Philip's demise and a number of them actually rebelled, thinking that without him the Macedonian hegemony would collapse. But they had sorely underestimated his son Alexander. Soon they would learn that for them, Philip's untimely passing had brought about only one major change—the name of the Macedonian king.

CHAPTER 8

Alexander: Military Genius and Conqueror of Persia

According to ancient sources, one day in 356 B.C., just after he had captured the northern Aegean city of Potidaea, the ambitious Macedonian conqueror Philip II received three pieces of good news on the same day. "The first," according to Plutarch,

This bust of Alexander III of Macedonia presently rests in the Archaeological Museum in the northern Greek city of Thessaloniki.

was that his general Parmenio had overcome the Illyrians in a great battle, the second that his race-horse had won a victory in the Olympic games, and the third that Alexander had been born. Naturally, he was over-joyed at the news, and the soothsayers raised his spirits still higher by assuring him that the son whose birth coincided with three victories would him-self prove invincible.[122]

Later tradition also claimed that on the day of Alexander's birth the huge and renowned temple of the goddess Artemis, in the Greek city of Ephesus (in Asia Minor), burned to the ground.[123] It was no wonder the goddess's house was destroyed, some people joked, since she was so busy attending to Alexander's birth!

Omens and legends like these surrounded the lives and legacies of nearly all great and accomplished figures in ancient times. Yet none became more accomplished and legendary than Alexander III, Philip's eldest legitimate child, who ascended the Macedonian throne when his father was assassinated in 336. Alexander not only carried out the conquest of Persia that his father had planned, but went on to create the largest empire the world had yet seen. In the process he created new political and cultural horizons throughout the eastern Mediterranean and Near Eastern spheres. As noted historian Chester Starr puts it, Alexander's conquests were

> one of the greatest turning points in ancient history. . . . Under Alexander the Greeks and Macedonians overthrew the native political system of the Near East itself. In this tremendous expansion, Greek intellectual and artistic leaders were inspired to a new wave of cultural achievements which had great effects on neighboring peoples from Rome to India.[124]

Although he could not at the time foresee how extensively his deeds would alter the world he was born into, Alexander probably never doubted that he was destined to change the established order. He had a deep interest, perhaps even an obsession, with predestination, believing that certain special humans were fated by the gods to achieve great deeds and everlasting fame. And apparently he saw himself as semidivine, like the ancient Achilles (the central figure of Homer's *Iliad*), a larger-than-life hero with whom he identified. According to the second-century A.D. Greek historian Arrian, whose history is the principal surviving source about Alexander's campaigns, Alexander told his soldiers: "Those who endure hardship and danger are the ones who achieve glory; and the most gratifying thing is to live with courage and to die leaving behind eternal renown." [125] As evidenced by the enormous reputation he earned, both in life and in death, Alexander managed to transform this lofty ideal into reality.

Boyhood and Education

As a royal prince growing up in the turbulent years when his father was extending Macedonian power throughout northern Greece, Alexander was naturally eager to accompany his father on his campaigns. But Philip forbade this, insisting that the boy's time for action and glory would come later, when he was more mature. As Plutarch tells it, Alexander remained impatient to see military action and as a result became increasingly jealous of Philip's successes:

Whenever he heard that Philip had captured some famous city or won an overwhelming victory, Alexander would show no pleasure at the news, but would declare to his friends, "Boys, my father will forestall me in everything. There will be nothing great or spectacular for you and me to show the world." He cared nothing for pleasure or wealth but only for deeds of valor and glory, and this was why he believed that the more he received from his father, the less would be left for him to conquer.[126]

Though eager to leave the Macedonian capital of Pella and see action, Alexander was an energetic and accomplished student who readily absorbed various elements of Greek culture. He eventually came to admire not only Homer's works, but also the tragedies of the great fifth-century B.C. Athenian playwrights. Furthermore, in his early teenage years he held frequent music and poetry-reading contests. In this period Alexander had many nurses and teachers, all supervised by a stern disciplinarian named Leonidas, a relative of his mother, Olympias.

Later, however, Plutarch tells us, Philip "considered that the task of training and educating his son was too important to be entrusted to the ordinary run of teachers . . . so he sent for Aristotle, the most famous and learned of the philosophers of his time." [127] Aristotle tutored Alexander for about three years beginning in 343, teaching him political science, ethics, and literature. The boy also received from Aristotle a copy of the *Iliad* that the great scholar-philosopher had edited himself; Alexander is said to have kept it with him for the rest of his life.

Early Tests of Skill and Resolve

The base of a ruined colon-nade (row of columns) in the palace at Aegae, where Alexander resided when visiting that city.

Aristotle no doubt taught Alexander a great deal; but the boy was, by all accounts, already wise beyond his years before his famous tutor arrived. Plutarch tells how once when Philip was away, a group of ambassadors from the Persian king arrived in Pella and Alexander received them in his father's stead. They were so im-

Aristotle (at right) instructs Alexander. The famous Athenian philosopher gave the young man a copy of Homer's Iliad, *which Alexander treasured.*

pressed by him that "they came away convinced that Philip's celebrated powers of perception were as nothing compared to the adventurous spirit and lofty ambitions of his son." [128]

Perhaps based on such examples of his son's abilities, when Alexander was sixteen Philip finally gave him a taste of the action he had been longing for. On leaving for a campaign, Philip bestowed on him the title of regent, actually allowing him to run the country on a temporary basis. Alexander quickly proved that he was indeed extraordinarily capable, despite his youth, by putting down an Illyrian rebellion and founding a new city, Alexandropolis. Just two years later (338 B.C.), the young man, now eighteen, faced a far more difficult test when his father placed him in charge of the Macedonian cavalry in the Battle of Chaeronea. There, Alexander charged his horsemen into a fatal gap that had opened in the allied lines and soon helped to surround and annihilate the Theban Sacred Band, the only allied contingent that stood its ground against the Macedonian onslaught.

In 336, when Alexander was twenty, his time of testing was cut short by Philip's assassination. Sooner than he had expected, the young man had to take his father's place as king of Macedonia and captain-general of the new Greek confederacy Philip had forged. But Alexander at once demonstrated that he was more than up to the task by the way he handled his first major crisis. Less than a year after he took power, Thebes made the mistake of rebelling against his authority. The Theban rebels stormed the

Alexander's father, Philip, is assassinated at Aegae. After slaying the killer, Alexander ascended the Macedonian throne.

Macedonian garrison then occupying their acropolis; but the besieged men managed to hold out for the short time it took Alexander to arrive. Perhaps to serve notice on all the Greeks that he would not tolerate such defiance, the young king punished Thebes harshly. He ordered every building in the city leveled, except for the temples (so that no one could accuse him of sacrilege) and the house of the poet Pindar, whose verses he admired. The Macedonians killed some six thousand Thebans and sold another thirty thousand, mostly women and children, into slavery.

Alexander's Military and Political Tactics

Having established himself as a ruler to be feared, in 334 B.C. Alexander initiated the great military campaigns that brought all the lands stretching from Greece to India under his authority. When he crossed the Hellespont into Asia Minor in the spring of that year, his army consisted of about thirty-two thousand infantry and five thousand cavalry.[129] At first glance this might seem a hopelessly inadequate force to pit against the mighty Persian Empire, which could field armies of two hundred thousand or more troops.

But Alexander was confident in his soldiers' abilities. He knew that, beginning with the legendary encounter at Marathon in 490, Greek hoplites had time and again proven themselves superior to

Persian fighters. Moreover, he now commanded the formidable phalanx and cavalry that had defeated the Greeks at Chaeronea. "Alexander's greatest asset," J. F. C. Fuller suggests, "was the army he inherited from his father; without it, in spite of his genius, his conquests would be inconceivable—it was an instrument exactly suited to his craft." [130]

Alexander was also supremely confident in his own abilities. And indeed, history has shown that his genius as a military strategist was his other great asset. Whether or not he was a more gifted general than his father is a matter for academic debate. What is certain is that in his Asian campaigns Alexander employed Philip's army and battlefield tactics brilliantly, often innovating as he went along and thereby improving on those tactics. The son also further developed the already effective siege techniques he had learned from his father. In F. E. Adcock's words, Alexander "pressed his sieges home with fiery and resourceful determination. No city, however strong, and no fort, however defended by art and nature, foiled his skillful attack." [131]

Of equal importance was Alexander's shrewd grasp of political manipulation (another skill learned at least in part from Philip), especially his ability to gain the allegiance of conquered peoples and thereby secure his gains. As part of his overall strategy in western Persia, for example, he freed the Greek cities he found under Persian domination and granted them self-determination. This was not based on any particular admiration or respect for democracy, for he was an absolute monarch to his core. Rather, he wisely perceived that the Persian king maintained influence over the Greek cities in Asia Minor through tyrants and ruling councils imposed on those cities by local Persian governors. Most of these Greeks believed in democracy and despised such Persian dictators; so by offering them not only freedom, but also self-determination, Alexander could and did win their allegiance.

Alexander employed a similar strategy of making friends with the non-Greek cities and peoples he encountered as he made his way across the Persian Empire. As Fuller points out,

> he decided to enter into alliance with every anti-Persian faction he contacted, irrespective of their political outlook, and with their aid create an inner front which, as he advanced, would progressively destroy the Persian imperium and leave a friendly country in his rear. Besides this, by winning over city by city, particularly the coastal cities, he would deprive the Persian fleet of its bases and thereby restrict its operations against his sea communications. [132]

The Conquest of Persia

Alexander clearly demonstrated the superiority of his army and personal talents in a long series of victories. His first major victory came only a few weeks after he had crossed the Hellespont. At the Granicus River, in northwestern Asia Minor, he came up against an army commanded by some of the local Persian governors, who had gathered their forces to block his path. Here is Arrian's exciting account of the battle's opening moments:

> There was a profound hush as both armies stood for a while motionless on the bank of the river, as if in awe of what was to come. Then Alexander . . . at the head of the right wing of the army, with the trumpets blaring and the shout going up to the God of Battle, moved forward into the river. . . . The leading files [of the phalanx] were met as they gained the river bank by volleys of missiles from the Persians, who kept up a continuous fire into the river. . . . A hand-to-hand struggle developed, the Macedonian mounted troops trying to force their way out of the water, the Persians doing their utmost to prevent them. Persian lances flew thick and fast, the long Macedonian spears thrust and stabbed. In this first onslaught Alexander's men, heavily outnumbered, suffered severely. . . . It was a cavalry battle with, as it were, infantry tactics: horse against horse, man against man, locked together; the Macedonians did their utmost to thrust the enemy once

A modern drawing of the battle at the Granicus River, in Asia Minor, Alexander's first victory over the Persians.

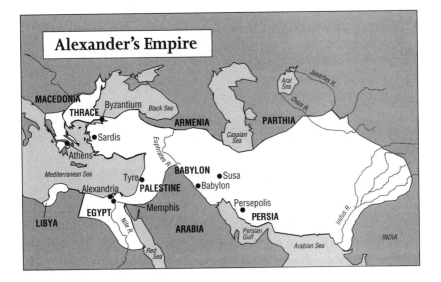

Alexander's Empire

and for all back from the river-bank and force him into open ground, while the Persians fought to prevent the landings or hurl their opponents back into the water.[133]

Eventually, the Macedonians won the day. Their losses were only about one or two hundred, compared to perhaps six or seven thousand for the enemy.

Alexander then marched southward and in the following year (333 B.C.), at Issus, in Syria, met a much larger Persian army, this one commanded by the Persian king, Darius III. The Persians lost again, and Darius escaped. Continuing southward, the Macedonians next entered Palestine, where they besieged the island city of Tyre. The Tyrians held out for seven months but finally succumbed after the Greeks built a massive earthen causeway to connect the island to the mainland. Then, in 332, Alexander liberated Egypt, which had been under Persian rule for two centuries. He established a new city in the Nile Delta, naming it Alexandria after himself. (Alexandria subsequently became one of the ancient world's greatest commercial and cultural centers.)

In the fall of 331, Alexander turned northeastward and penetrated the heart of the Persian Empire. At Gaugamela (or Arbela), near the Tigris River in what is now Iraq, Darius failed once again to stop him, losing over forty thousand men in the attempt. The Persian monarch made good another escape but was murdered by some of his own officers shortly afterward.[134] After the battle, Alexander occupied the three Persian capitals—Babylon, Susa, and Persepolis—none of which offered any resistance.

As Alexander lies dying, his troops pay their last respects. Supposedly, when asked to whom he left his realm, he answered, "the strongest."

The End of the Road

Not satisfied with subduing the world's largest existing realm, Alexander continued eastward, eventually reaching India. There, in 326 B.C., at the Hydapses River, he defeated a large Indian army equipped with some two hundred battle elephants, at the time a frightening novelty in Western warfare. He might have gone on to conquer all of India; however, his exhausted troops, many of whom had not seen home and family in many years, mutinied and demanded that he turn back.

This proved to be the end of the road for Alexander. Shortly after returning to Persia, he died, possibly of malaria, in Babylon on June 10, 323. He was only thirty-three. That someone so young accomplished so much in so short a span has surrounded his name with an air of almost superstitious awe ever since. Arrian expressed it this way:

> Never in all the world was there another like him, and therefore I cannot but feel that some power more than human was concerned in his birth . . . and there is the further evidence of the extraordinary way in which he is held, as no mere man could be, in honor and remembrance.[135]

CHAPTER 9

Pyrrhus: Soldier of Fortune in a Chaotic Age

Pyrrhus, whose name means "fiery," was one of the most important of the many minor monarchs and military adventurers who proliferated in the Hellenistic Age. He was a product of and a major player in the *Diadochi* wars, the long and chaotic conflicts in which Alexander's successors, their sons, and others fought one another for dominance in the eastern Mediterranean world. No clear overall winner emerged from these desperate struggles. The result was the establishment of several successor kingdoms, which alternately fought or aided one another. Shifting political alliances, back-stabbing, naked military aggression, and the ready availability of mercenary generals became the hallmarks of the age.

In his often colorful career, Pyrrhus involved himself in all of these activities. A king of Epirus, the small kingdom of northwestern Greece from which Alexander's mother, Olympias, had hailed, he fought both with and against several of the major successors to Alexander and their sons. Hired to go to Italy and fight the Romans, he was the first Greek general to do so, managing to defeat them on more than one occasion. And for a short while, it seemed that he might seize complete control of the Macedonian kingdom.

But though he was a gifted military tactician, Pyrrhus, like other Hellenistic monarchs, lacked the patience and long-range judgment necessary to create political stability. In the end, his vast expenditures of energy and talent, both in Italy and Greece, came to nothing. In a way, his weaknesses and failures symbolized and foreshadowed the ultimate failure of the Hellenistic realms. Like Pyrrhus, they underestimated the Romans and failed to mount a coordinated, consistent, and long-term offensive against them, eventually causing both their own undoing and the end of Greek rule in the ancient world.

Pyrrhus was born in 319 B.C. of illustrious ancestry. His family connection with Olympias made him Alexander's second cousin.

And the Epirote royal house also claimed descent from Achilles via the legendary hero's son, Neoptolemus (who was also sometimes called Pyrrhus). According to local tradition, after the Trojan War Neoptolemus settled in Epirus and founded its ruling dynasty.

From the start, Pyrrhus's life proved unstable and fraught with danger. When he was just an infant, his father, Aeacides, was deposed during a civil conflict and had to flee the country. Friends of the family whisked the young prince to safety, eventually taking him to the nearby kingdom of Illyria. There, the local king, Glaucias, raised Pyrrhus as one of his own children. According to Plutarch, the king took a liking to the boy and

> a little later, when Pyrrhus's enemies demanded that he should be handed over to them . . . Glaucias refused to give him up. Indeed, after Pyrrhus had reached the age of twelve, Glaucias actually invaded Epirus with an army and set him on the throne there.[136]

Pyrrhus reigned as a minor in Epirus from 307 to 302. During these years he allied himself with Demetrius I of Macedonia, who became known as Poliorcetes, "the Besieger." Demetrius (born 336) was the son of Alexander's general Antigonus. A field commander and admiral under his father, Demetrius had long been involved in Antigonus's fruitless attempts to reunite Alexander's empire under Macedonian rule (specifically Antigonid rule, since

Pyrrhus (the infant held up in foreground) is saved by family friends during a civil conflict in the kingdom of Epirus.

Antigonus considered himself Alexander's sole heir). In 307, the year Pyrrhus acquired the Epirote throne, Demetrius captured Athens from another of Alexander's generals, Cassander. (Cassander had earlier seized control of Greece and executed Olympias and some of Alexander's other relatives.) The following year Demetrius decisively defeated still another of the *Diadochi*, Ptolemy I, ruler of Egypt. These victories made Demetrius and Antigonus seem, at least for the moment, to be the most powerful men around. So when Pyrrhus allied himself with their royal house and married off his sister to Demetrius, Pyrrhus's prestige rose and his throne appeared secure.

A modern drawing of Demetrius, the Besieger, who at first befriended Pyrrhus but later became his bitter enemy.

However, when the young Epirote king was seventeen, his own people rebelled, forcing him into a second exile. Having nowhere else to turn, he ran to Demetrius, who advised him and gave him a high-ranking position in his army. The following year (301), Pyrrhus fought alongside Demetrius and Antigonus in the huge Battle of Ipsus (in Asia Minor), where the Antigonids were defeated and Antigonus himself was slain.

A New Change of Fortunes

Having attached himself to men who had turned out to be major losers, and still exiled from his native land, Pyrrhus did not appear to have a promising future. But in short order, his fortunes once more took a positive turn. The kingdomless Demetrius made a treaty with his old enemy Ptolemy and sent Pyrrhus to Egypt as a hostage to seal the bargain. There, says Plutarch, the young man "gave Ptolemy ample proof of his prowess and endurance both in hunting and in military exercises." [137] Ptolemy came to regard Pyrrhus so highly, in fact, that in 299 B.C. he joined the young man, then twenty, in marriage with his stepdaughter Antigone. About two years later, Ptolemy supplied the money and troops Pyrrhus needed to win back Epirus. "Many of the Epirotes welcomed his arrival," recalls Plutarch, for they had come to hate Neoptolemus [II, the current king], who had proved himself a harsh and repressive ruler. Pyrrhus was afraid, however, that if he drove out his rival, Neoptolemus might turn for help to one of the other successors to Alexander, and so he made a pact with him, whereby they agreed to share the royal power.[138]

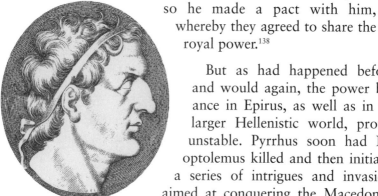

Ptolemy I, one of the Diadochi, *became ruler of Egypt and Pyrrhus's father-in-law.*

But as had happened before, and would again, the power balance in Epirus, as well as in the larger Hellenistic world, proved unstable. Pyrrhus soon had Neoptolemus killed and then initiated a series of intrigues and invasions aimed at conquering the Macedonian kingdom. This brought him to death grips with his old friend Demetrius, who then controlled that realm (having seized it after Cassander's death). For a short while, Pyrrhus was successful and held control of most of western Greece. In 285, however, Lysimachus, another of the *Diadochi*, who had wrested Macedonia from Demetrius, drove Pyrrhus back into Epirus.

Pyrrhic Victories

Undaunted, the resilient and enterprising Pyrrhus soon embarked on the Italian military adventure for which he is famous. The equally enterprising Romans had recently come into possession of much of the Italian peninsula, and had begun to threaten the Greek cities that had for several centuries dotted southern Italy.[139] The most important of these was prosperous Tarentum (its Latin name; the Greeks called it Taras), located in the "instep" of the Italian boot. In 282 B.C., tensions between the Romans and Tarentines came to a head when the latter sank a small fleet of Roman ships that had violated Tarentum's territorial waters. The Tarentines fully realized that Rome would respond in kind and soon appealed for aid to the nearest and already one of the most renowned Greek soldiers of fortune—Pyrrhus.

Pyrrhus accepted the invitation. He was likely motivated by more than sympathy for fellow Greeks and the opportunity for a good fight. Plutarch attributes the following remarks to him (which Pyrrhus may never have actually said, but which probably summarize what he was thinking at the time):

> If we can conquer the Romans, there is no other Greek or barbarian city which is a match for us. We shall straight-away become the masters of the whole of Italy. . . . After Italy, [we will take] Sicily, of course. . . . The place posi-tively beckons to us. It is rich, well-populated, and easy to capture. . . . We can make it the spring-board for much greater enterprises. How could we resist making an at-tempt upon Libya and Carthage? . . . And when we have conquered these countries, none of our enemies who are so insolent to us now will be able to stand up to us.[140]

Driven by these dreams of conquest, in the spring of 280 Pyrrhus crossed from Greece to Italy with a force of some 22,500 men and twenty Indian war elephants. He fought his first battle against the Roman legions at Heraclea, not far from Tarentum. The Roman troops had never seen elephants before and their horses were terrified by the huge beasts, so Pyrrhus's forces man-aged to kill over 7,000 of their op-ponents and score a victory. But it was a costly victory, for the Ro-mans proved to be stubborn and courageous fighters and slew some 4,000 of Pyrrhus's men, over a sixth of his army.

Pyrrhus then boldly marched on Rome. He got within forty miles of the city, but soon decided to turn back when it became obvious that Rome's local Italian allies were not going to come over to his side. Without their help, he knew, it would be impossible to take and hold such a large and well-fortified city. He fought the Romans again the following year (279) at Auscu-

An idealized depiction of Pyr-rhus as a young soldier. Later in life, he was unable to defeat the Romans decisively.

lum, in southeastern Italy. Again, he won; but this time his losses were so great that he is said to have quipped: "One more victory like that over the Romans will destroy us completely!"[141] Ever since, an excessively costly win has been called a Pyrrhic victory.

At this point, Pyrrhus abruptly decided to try his luck in Sicily. There, he probably reasoned, he could defeat and expel the Carthaginians and, with Sicily's resources and manpower at his disposal, conduct a successful campaign against both Rome and Carthage. But in the three years he spent in Sicily, he fared no better than he had in Italy. In 275 he returned to Italy, fought one more costly battle against the Romans, and then decided to cut his losses. On leaving for Epirus, he supposedly made the perceptive remark: "My friends, what a wrestling ground we are leaving behind us for the Romans and Carthaginians." [142] (Eleven years later, Rome and Carthage locked horns in the First Punic War, the most destructive conflict the world had yet seen.)

The Assessment of History

Pyrrhus had no sooner reached home than he launched still another aggressive campaign. This time the goal was to reverse his former losses in Macedonia and seize control of that kingdom from its present ruler, Antigonus II, Demetrius's son. By 273 B.C., Pyrrhus had made impressive gains and seemed on the brink of fulfilling his goal. But then, in another abrupt and ill-considered change of focus, he headed southward and initiated a new military adventure in Sparta. A year later, in a street fight in Argos (in the northeastern Peloponnesus), he was killed when a roof tile thrown by an old woman struck him in the head.

Pyrrhus's fame rests mainly on his abilities as a soldier and battlefield tactician. Because surviving ancient texts provide little detail about his battles, it is difficult for modern scholars to judge just

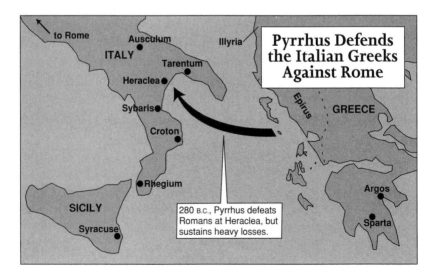

Pyrrhus Defends the Italian Greeks Against Rome

to Rome · Ausculum · ITALY · Tarentum · Illyria · Heraclea · Sybaris · Croton · Rhegium · SICILY · Syracuse · Epirus · GREECE · Argos · Sparta

280 B.C., Pyrrhus defeats Romans at Heraclea, but sustains heavy losses.

how great a general he actually was. But there is no doubt that the ancients considered him one of the greatest. According to the first-century B.C. Roman historian Livy, when Hannibal of Carthage, himself one of the three or four best generals of antiquity, was asked to choose the greatest, he ranked Pyrrhus above himself and second only to Alexander.[143]

Pyrrhus fares a good deal worse in assessments of his overall strategy, judgment, and success. Modern scholars generally agree with Plutarch's astute evaluation, that

> what he won through his feats of arms he lost by indulging in vain hopes; and through his obsessive desire to seize what lay beyond his grasp, he constantly failed to secure what lay within it. For this reason Antigonus compared him to a player at dice, who makes many good throws, but does not understand how to exploit them when they are made.[144]

The leading citizens of a Greek city bow to Roman troops who have captured the town. Rome eventually subdued all of Greece.

Ultimately, Pyrrhus's weaknesses overcame his strengths and led to his premature downfall. The same can be said of Greek leaders in the next few generations. As a result of their imprudent policies, during the century that followed his passing the Roman eagle's huge wings stretched inexorably outward, completely and permanently enfolding the Greek world.

NOTES

Introduction: Greece's Pivotal Movers and Shakers

1. Michael Grant, *The Classical Greeks*. New York: Scribner's, 1989, p. xi.

2. C. M. Bowra, *Classical Greece*. New York: Time-Life Books, 1965, pp. 11, 18.

3. Grant, *The Classical Greeks*, p. 263.

Chapter 1: A Brief History of Ancient Greece

4. Herodotus *The Histories* 8.140, trans. Aubrey de Sélincourt. New York: Penguin Books, 1972, pp. 572–73.

5. Herodotus *The Histories* 8.144, Sélincourt translation, pp. 574–75.

6. Thomas R. Martin, *Ancient Greece: From Prehistoric to Hellenistic Times*. New Haven, CT: Yale University Press, 1996, p. 16.

7. For analyses of the various theories, see Robert Drews, *The Coming of the Greeks: Indo-European Conquests in the Aegean and Near East*. Princeton, NJ: Princeton University Press, 1988. A useful overview of Mycenaean civilization is William Taylor, *The Mycenaeans*. London: Thames and Hudson, 1983.

8. Bowra, *Classical Greece*, p. 31.

9. In the story, the young Athenians were sacrificed to the Minotaur, a creature half-man and half-bull. Theseus slew the beast and released the prisoners. The Minotaur was likely a garbled memory of Minoan priests, who, some evidence suggests, wore bull masks when performing sacrifices.

10. The theory that the catastrophic eruption of the volcano on the small island of Thera, just north of Crete, caused the demise of Minoan civilization is unproven. The most recent calculations date the eruption to circa 1628 B.C., too early to account for the damage done to Minoan palaces circa 1400. However, the evidence is quite convincing that the eruption and its destruction of the thriving Minoan community on Thera gave rise to the legend of the lost city of Atlantis. See Charles Pellegrino, *Unearthing Atlantis: An Archaeological Odyssey*. New York: Random House, 1991, and Rodney Castleden, *Atlantis Destroyed*. New York: Routledge, 1998.

11. Michael Grant, *The Rise of the Greeks*. New York: Macmillan, 1987, p. 147.

12. For an overview of these theories, see Robert Drews, *The End of the Bronze Age: Changes in Warfare and the Catastrophe of ca.1200 B.C.* Princeton, NJ: Princeton University Press, 1993. Drews himself contends that military innovations among the peoples living on the periphery of the Mediterranean world allowed them to defeat the chariot corps of the Bronze Age kingdoms.

13. There were apparently some exceptions to this scenario. Recent archaeological evidence shows that a settlement at Lefkandi, on the western shore of Euboea (the large island lying along the eastern coast of the Greek mainland) enjoyed considerable prosperity in this period. Such sites remain unusual, however, and perhaps represent rare and relatively short-lived surviving pockets of Mycenaean culture.

14. Victor D. Hanson, *The Other Greeks: The Family Farm and the Agrarian Roots of Western Civilization*. New York: Simon and Schuster, 1995, p. 114.

15. Hanson, *The Other Greeks*, p. 31.

16. Hanson, *The Other Greeks*, p. 222.

17. At first, Athens's wealth derived partly from trade and partly from the large quantities of silver that flowed from its mines at Laurium, in southern Attica. Later, the Athenians gained and exploited for their own purposes huge amounts of revenue in the form of tribute (payment acknowledging submission) from the member states of its maritime empire.

18. Plutarch *Life of Pericles* 13, in *The Rise and Fall of Athens: Nine Greek Lives by Plutarch*, trans. Ian Scott-Kilvert. New York: Penguin, 1960, p. 179.

19. Thucydides *Peloponnesian War* 2.8.1, published as *The Landmark Thucydides: A Comprehensive Guide to the Peloponnesian War*, trans. Richard Crawley, ed. Robert B. Strassler. New York: Simon and Schuster, 1996, p. 93.

20. Xenophon *Hellenica* 7.5.27, published as *A History of My Times*, trans. Rex Warner. New York: Penguin Books, 1979, p. 403.

21. Quoted in Polybius *The Histories* 5.104, in *Polybius: The Rise of the Roman Empire*, trans. Ian Scott-Kilvert. New York: Penguin Books, 1979, pp. 299–300.

22. Naphtali Lewis, *Life in Egypt Under Roman Rule*. Oxford: Clarendon Press, 1983, p. 10.

Chapter 2: Solon: Lawgiver and Social Reformer

23. Quoted in Plutarch *Life of Solon* 18, in *Rise and Fall of Athens*, p. 60.

24. The other six sages were: scientist and philosopher Thales of Miletus; elected ruler and lawgiver Pittacus of Mytilene; judge and diplomat Bias of Priene; benevolent and popular tyrant Cleobulus of Lindus; community elder and statesman Chilon of Sparta; and benevolent tyrant and public builder Periander of Corinth. The later famous story (cited by Plutarch in *Solon* 3–7, in *Rise and Fall of Athens*, pp. 45–49), in which the seven men know one another, banquet together, and strive to "outdo one another in modesty and goodwill" is undoubtedly fanciful.

25. Plutarch *Life of Solon* 2, in *Rise and Fall of Athens*, p. 44.

26. But Athens did not acquire permanent control of Salamis until sometime in the late sixth century B.C., when Sparta arbitrated the dispute.

27. Quoted in Kathleen Freeman, *The Work and Life of Solon, with a Translation of His Poems*. Cardiff: University of Wales Press, 1926. Reprint, New York: Arno, 1976, p. 207.

28. Aristotle *The Athenian Constitution* 3.6, in *Aristotle: The Athenian Constitution, Eudemian Ethics, Virtues and Vices*, trans. H. Rackham. 1952. Reprint, Cambridge, MA: Harvard University Press, 1996, p. 19.

29. Plutarch *Solon* 14, in *Rise and Fall of Athens*, p. 55.

30. Quoted in Freeman, *Work and Life of Solon*, p. 214.

31. Aristotle *The Athenian Constitution* 6.1, Rackham translation, pp. 23–25.

32. Quoted in Kenneth J. Atchity, ed., *The Classical Greek Reader*. New York: Oxford University Press, 1996, p. 57. It is uncertain how Solon carried out these measures, but it is probable that he used state money to buy back those in slavery and sent agents to seek out and bring back those in exile.

33. Plutarch *Solon* 18, in *Rise and Fall of Athens*, pp. 59–60.

34. Grant, *Rise of the Greeks*, p. 52.

35. Some modern scholars have suggested that attributing the invention of the Council to Solon was a later fabrication (for a

summary of this argument, see Victor Ehrenberg, *From Solon to Socrates*. London: Methuen, 1968, p. 66); however, the tradition that Solon invented it was so strong only a century later, it seems likely to have had some basis in fact.

36. Grant, *Rise of the Greeks*, p. 53.

37. Plutarch *Solon* 16, 26, in *Rise and Fall of Athens*, pp. 58, 68.

38. Quoted in Freeman, *Work and Life of Solon*, p. 216.

39. Plato *Timaeus* 23, in *The Dialogues of Plato*, trans. Benjamin Jowett. Great Books of the Western World. Chicago: Encyclopaedia Britannica, 1952, p. 445.

40. Quoted in Atchity, *Classical Greek Reader*, pp. 57–58.

Chapter 3: Themistocles: Father of Athenian Naval Supremacy

41. Thucydides *Peloponnesian War* 1.138.3, in *The Landmark Thucydides*, p. 79.

42. The Roman biographer Cornelius Nepos claims (in *Themistocles* 1.2) that she was a native of Acarnania (a region of western Greece) who became an Athenian citizen after moving to Athens. (It should be remembered that for a Greek woman citizenship did not include civic rights such as voting and holding office.)

43. Plutarch *Themistocles* 1, in *Rise and Fall of Athens*, p. 77.

44. Herodotus *The Histories* 5.66, Sélincourt translation, p. 364.

45. A. J. Podlecki, *The Life of Themistocles*. Montreal: McGill-Queen's University Press, 1975, p. 7.

46. While Themistocles was archon, the playwright Phrynichus wrote and produced *The Capture of Miletus*. Many Athenians deeply regretted that they had not done something to help the Milesians (with whom they had long maintained strong ties). According to Herodotus, "the audience in the theater burst into tears," after which "the author was fined a thousand drachmas for reminding them of a disaster which touched them so closely, and they forbade anybody ever to put the play on the stage again" (*The Histories* 6.20, Sélincourt translation, p. 395).

47. Podlecki, *Life of Themistocles*, p. 9.

48. Plutarch *Themistocles* 3, in *Rise and Fall of Athens*, p. 80.

49. Herodotus *The Histories* 7.144, Sélincourt translation, p. 490. Because most of his countrymen did not yet perceive the Persians as a threat, he claimed the ships were needed to fight the

nearby island polis of Aegina, which Athens had been fighting on and off for some time. But it is almost certain that in Themistocles' mind the Persians loomed as a far larger threat.

50. Plutarch *Themistocles* 4, in *Rise and Fall of Athens*, p. 81.

51. These estimates are by modern historians and military experts. Herodotus's figures, including 1,750,000 infantry, 100,000 mounted troops, 510,000 sailors, and over 2 million camp personnel, are hugely exaggerated, for so gigantic a host could not have sustained itself on the march.

52. Quoted in Herodotus *The Histories* 7.141, Sélincourt translation, pp. 488–89.

53. Considering when the prophecy was given, in late 481 or early 480 B.C., several months before anyone had any idea where the naval showdown with the Persians would take place, the reference to "divine Salamis" is suspicious. It may well be the result of Themistocles' later manipulation of the oracle to make his victory at Salamis appear divinely destined, although no solid evidence for such trickery has yet been found.

54. Quoted in R. J. Leonardon, *The Saga of Themistocles*. London: Thames and Hudson, 1978, pp. 69–70. These words come from an inscription discovered in Troezen in 1959. Some scholars think it is a later copy of the actual decree, while others suspect it is a forgery. Even if it is a fake, though, it likely captures the spirit, if not the actual wording, of the original.

55. Herodotus, *The Histories* 8.60–61, Sélincourt translation, pp. 543–44.

56. Aeschylus *The Persians* 416–30, in *Aeschylus: Prometheus Bound, The Suppliants, Seven Against Thebes, The Persians*, trans. Philip Vellacott. Baltimore: Penguin Books, 1961, p. 134.

57. *Themistocles* 6, in Cornelius Nepos, *The Book of the Great Generals of Foreign Nations*, trans. John C. Rolfe. Cambridge, MA: Harvard University Press, 1960, p. 397.

58. Thucydides *Peloponnesian War* 1.138.6, in *The Landmark Thucydides*, p. 79.

59. Podlecki, *Life of Themistocles*, p. 44.

Chapter 4: Pericles: Athens's Guide to Its Greatest Age

60. Quoted in Thucydides, *The Peloponnesian War* 2.41.4, trans. Rex Warner. New York: Penguin Books, 1972, p. 148.

61. Plutarch *Life of Pericles* 15, in *Rise and Fall of Athens*, p. 183.

62. Plutarch *Life of Pericles* 15, in *Rise and Fall of Athens*, p. 183.

63. Donald Kagan, *Life of Pericles of Athens and the Birth of Democracy*. New York: Free Press, 1991, pp. 6–7.

64. Plutarch *Life of Pericles* 5, in *Rise and Fall of Athens*, p. 169.

65. Plutarch *Life of Pericles* 3, in *Rise and Fall of Athens*, p. 167.

66. Aristotle *The Athenian Constitution* 25.2, Rackham translation, pp. 75–77.

67. Aristotle names one Aristodicus of Tanagra (about whom nothing is known) as the assassin. Other ancient writers claim that the identity of the murderer(s) remained a mystery.

68. Donald Kagan, *The Outbreak of the Peloponnesian War*. Ithaca, NY: Cornell University Press, 1969, p. 87.

69. Charles A. Robinson, *Athens in the Age of Pericles*. Norman: University of Oklahoma Press, 1959, p. 90. It must be remembered, however, that only free males exercised full citizenship rights. Women, slaves, and resident foreigners (*metics*) were excluded from the Assembly and holding public office.

70. Thucydides *Peloponnesian War* 2.43.1, in *The Landmark Thucydides*, p. 115.

71. Peter Green, *The Parthenon*. New York: Newsweek Book Division, 1973, p. 71.

72. Plutarch *Life of Pericles* 12, in *Rise and Fall of Athens*, p. 177.

73. John Miliadis, *The Acropolis*. Athens: M. Pechlivanidis, n.d., p. 14.

74. Peter Levi, *Atlas of the Greek World*. New York: Facts On File, 1984, p. 140.

75. Thucydides claims (in *Peloponnesian War* 1.104) that the Athenians sent 200 ships, which would mean a force of some 40,000 men, including sailors. Modern historians suggest a much smaller number, however—possibly 40 ships and 8,000 men. For a detailed discussion of the evidence, see Russell Meiggs, *The Athenian Empire*. Oxford: Clarendon Press, 1972, pp. 101–108.

76. Kagan, *Outbreak*, p. 97.

77. Quoted in Plutarch *Life of Pericles* 28, in *Rise and Fall of Athens*, p. 194.

78. The specific charge was that, in carving a scene on the shield of the huge statue of Athena that stood inside the Parthenon,

Phidias included among the human figures two who bore a suspicious resemblance to himself and Pericles. No one had ever before portrayed specific contemporary people on a sacred shrine and some Athenians feared that doing so might insult the goddess.

79. Plutarch *Life of Pericles* 29, in *Rise and Fall of Athens*, p. 196.

80. Quoted in Thucydides *Peloponnesian War* 1.143.5, in *The Landmark Thucydides*, p. 83.

Chapter 5: Alcibiades: Beloved Rogue and Infamous Traitor

81. Plutarch *Life of Alcibiades* 2, in *Rise and Fall of Athens*, p. 246.

82. Nepos *Alcibiades* 1, in *Book of the Great Generals*, Rolfe translation, p. 437.

83. Thucydides *Peloponnesian War* 6.15.4, in *The Landmark Thucydides*, p. 370.

84. Plutarch *Life of Alcibiades* 1, in *Rise and Fall of Athens*, pp. 245–46.

85. Plutarch *Life of Alcibiades* 16, in *Rise and Fall of Athens*, p. 258.

86. Plutarch *Life of Alcibiades* 7, in *Rise and Fall of Athens*, p. 251. The battle was fought near the city of Potidaea, on the northern coast of the Aegean. A member of the Delian League, the city had recently (434 B.C.) rebelled against Athenian authority and sought aid from Corinth. Two years later, a force of two thousand Athenian hoplites, Alcibiades and Socrates among them, defeated a smaller Corinthian army in the battle in question. The incident contributed, along with other factors, to the outbreak of the Peloponnesian War in 431.

87. Thucydides provides a detailed summary of the events leading up to the battle, as well as the fighting itself, in *Peloponnesian War* 5.43–5.74 (see *The Landmark Thucydides*, pp. 327–46).

88. Quoted in Thucydides *Peloponnesian War* 6.20.2–4, in *The Landmark Thucydides*, p. 373.

89. Quoted in Thucydides *Peloponnesian War* 6.17.2–6, 6.18.4–6, in *The Landmark Thucydides*, pp. 371–73.

90. Thucydides *Peloponnesian War* 6.24.4, in *The Landmark Thucydides*, p. 375.

91. The statues, called Herms, which consisted of busts resting atop stone posts bearing sculpted replicas of erect male genitalia,

stood as guardians at doorways and street intersections. The genitalia of hundreds of them had been broken off. Another charge was that Alcibiades and his friends had mocked a solemn local religious ceremony. It is highly doubtful, however, that he was guilty of these crimes, since he was smart enough not to risk stirring up trouble on the eve of the venture that promised to bring him what he most wanted—power and glory.

92. Thucydides *Peloponnesian War* 7.87.6, in *The Landmark Thucydides*, p. 478.

93. Xenophon *Hellenica* 1.4.13–20, Warner translation, pp. 71–72.

94. Ehrenberg, *From Solon to Socrates*, p. 319.

Chapter 6: Epaminondas: Extraordinary Military Innovator and Strategist

95. Frank E. Adcock, *The Greek and Macedonian Art of War.* Berkeley and Los Angeles: University of California Press, 1957, p. 24.

96. Diodorus Siculus *Library of History* 15.88.1–4, trans. Charles L. Sherman and C. Bradford Welles. Cambridge, MA: Harvard University Press, 1963, vol. 7, pp. 197–99.

97. Grant, *Classical Greeks*, p. 197.

98. Faced with the arrival of a force of armed exiled Theban patriots and Athenian volunteers the next day, the Spartan troops holding the citadel withdrew, much to the embarrassment of Spartan leaders. Plutarch gives a detailed account of the coup and its aftermath in his *Life of Pelopidas* 7–14 (see *The Age of Alexander: Nine Greek Lives by Plutarch*, trans. Ian Scott-Kilvert. New York: Penguin, 1973, pp. 75–82).

99. Quoted in Plutarch, *Moralia* 592 F, in *Plutarch: Essays*, trans. Robin Waterfield. New York: Penguin Books, 1992, p. 346.

100. Plutarch *Life of Agesilaus* 27–28, in *Age of Alexander*, p. 54.

101. Perhaps roughly a tenth of these were Spartans; the rest were Peloponnesian allies.

102. Diodorus *Library of History* 15.52.1–2, vol. 7, p. 97.

103. Peter Connolly, *Greece and Rome at War.* London: Greenhill Books, 1998, p. 51.

104. Peter Connolly has speculated that Epaminondas also may have invented the use of the longer spear, or pike, in the phalanx (see *Greece and Rome at War*, p. 51). This innovation has traditionally been credited to Philip II, whose "Macedonian phalanx"

resembled a huge porcupine with its quills erect. Neither Diodorus nor Xenophon (nor any other ancient historian) mentions Epaminondas's Thebans using such pikes; but it is possible that at the time the degree of innovation was minor enough to have escaped notice. For instance, Epaminondas may have had the soldiers in the second file of his left wing use longer spears to make his new oblique formation slightly more lethal; if so, Philip later brilliantly built on the idea by having *all* members of his own phalanx carry pikes.

105. Diodorus *Library of History* 15.55.2–15.66.3, vol. 7, pp. 107–11.

106. Diodorus claims 20,000 foot and 2,000 horse for the Peloponnesians and 30,000 foot and 3,000 horse for the Boeotians. Xenophon is silent about the numbers of combatants.

107. Xenophon *Hellenica* 7.5.27, Warner translation, p. 403.

108. Diodorus *Library of History* 15.87.1, 5–6, vol. 7, pp. 195–97.

Chapter 7: Philip: Political Opportunist and Unifier of Greece

109. *Address to Philip*, quoted in Atchity, *Classical Greek Reader*, pp. 183, 186.

110. Grant, *Classical Greeks*, p. 240.

111. Peter Green, *Alexander of Macedon, 356–323 B.C.: A Historical Biography*. Berkeley and Los Angeles: University of California Press, 1991, p. 6.

112. Some modern scholars doubt that Philip acquired much, if any, important military information while in Thebes. See, for instance, J. R. Ellis, *Philip II and Macedonian Imperialism*. New York: Thames and Hudson, 1977, pp. 43–44. It stands to reason, however, that a young man of his intelligence and ambition, living in such close proximity with the leading generals of the day, would have learned as much as he could about their army.

113. Green, *Alexander of Macedon*, pp. 24–25.

114. Peter Connolly provides a detailed and very readable discussion of the Macedonian phalanx and its use by Philip and Alexander in his *Greece and Rome at War*, pp. 68–70.

115. Diodorus *Library of History* 16.95.2–4, vol. 8, p. 103.

116. David Hogarth, *Philip and Alexander of Macedon*. 1897. Reprint, Freeport, NY: Books for the Libraries Press, 1971, p. 64.

117. J. F. C. Fuller, *The Generalship of Alexander the Great*. New Brunswick, NJ: Rutgers University Press, 1960, p. 24.

118. Demosthenes *First Philippic,* in *Olynthiacs, Philippics, Minor Speeches*, trans, J. H. Vince. Cambridge, MA: Harvard University Press, 1962, pp. 73–75.

119. Plutarch *Life of Demosthenes* 18, in *Age of Alexander*, p. 203.

120. The Athenians realized that they were getting off easy. Even Demosthenes grudgingly admitted that Philip's offer was generous and accepted his terms. Philip had sound reasons for dealing leniently with Athens, the first being his genuine love and respect for the city's high culture. Perhaps more important, however, he respected Athens's formidable navy. Consisting of well over 300 ships, it was still intact and could prove a difficult and dangerous obstacle if he chose to invade Attica.

121. Green, *Alexander of Macedon*, p. 86.

Chapter 8: Alexander: Military Genius and Conqueror of Persia

122. Plutarch *Life of Alexander* 3, in *Age of Alexander*, p. 255.

123. The Temple at Ephesus, which was over four hundred feet long and featured a forest of columns, each some sixty feet tall, was later designated one of the seven wonders of the ancient world. For a detailed description, see Peter Clayton and Martin Price, eds., *The Seven Wonders of the Ancient World*. New York: Barnes and Noble, 1988, pp. 78–99.

124. Chester G. Starr, *A History of the Ancient World*. New York: Oxford University Press, 1991, p. 410.

125. Arrian *Anabasis Alexandri* 5.26, trans. Don Nardo.

126. Plutarch *Life of Alexander* 5, in *Age of Alexander*, p. 256.

127. Plutarch *Life of Alexander* 7, in *Age of Alexander*, p. 258.

128. Plutarch *Life of Alexander* 5, in *Age of Alexander*, p. 256.

129. Of the infantry, some 12,000 were Macedonians composing the phalanx, another 14,000 were hoplites and light-armed fighters from other allied Greek states, and the other 6,000 were archers and javelin men from the northern Aegean and the island of Crete. The cavalry broke down into roughly 2,000 Macedonian Companions, 1,800 expert Thessalian horsemen, and a mixture of smaller allied contingents. For more detail, see Nick Sekunda and John Warry, *Alexander the Great: His Armies and Campaigns, 334–323 B.C.* London: Osprey, 1998.

130. Fuller, *Generalship*, p. 292.

131. Adcock, *Greek and Macedonian Art of War*, p. 59.

132. Fuller, *Generalship*, p. 92.

133. Arrian *Anabasis* 1.15, published as *The Campaigns of Alexander*, trans. Aubrey de Sélincourt. New York: Penguin Books, 1971, pp. 72–73.

134. Alexander considered this a treacherous act and severely punished Bessus, the Persian nobleman who led the conspiracy. See Plutarch's *Life of Alexander* 44 (in *Age of Alexander*, pp. 300–301), Arrian's *Anabasis* 4.7–8 (in Sélincourt translation, pp. 212–13), and Quintus Curtius Rufus's *History of Alexander* 7.5.36–40, trans. John Yardley. New York: Penguin Books, 1984, p. 161.

135. Arrian *Anabasis* 7.30, Sélincourt translation, p. 398.

Chapter 9: Pyrrhus: Soldier of Fortune in a Chaotic Age

136. Plutarch *Life of Pyrrhus* 3, in *Age of Alexander*, p. 386.

137. Plutarch *Life of Pyrrhus* 4, in *Age of Alexander*, p. 387.

138. Plutarch *Life of Pyrrhus* 5, in *Age of Alexander*, p. 388.

139. These cities, including Sybaris, Croton, Rhegium, and Tarentum, among many others, had been established in an intensive burst of Greek colonization spanning the period circa 750–550 B.C. In Pyrrhus's day, some were larger, and all were more cultured, than Rome.

140. Quoted in Plutarch *Life of Pyrrhus* 14, in *Age of Alexander*, p. 399.

141. Quoted in Plutarch *Life of Pyrrhus* 21, in *Age of Alexander*, p. 409.

142. Quoted in Plutarch *Life of Pyrrhus* 23, in *Age of Alexander*, p. 412.

143. See Livy's *Roman History* 35.15, in *Livy: Rome and the Mediterranean*, trans. Henry Bettenson. New York: Penguin Books, 1976, pp. 208–209.

144. Plutarch *Life of Pyrrhus* 26, in *Age of Alexander*, p. 414.

CHRONOLOGY

B.C.
ca. 3000–1100
Greece's Bronze Age, in which people use tools and weapons made of bronze.

ca. 2000
People speaking an early form of Greek begin entering the Greek peninsula from the east or northeast.

ca. 1400
The Greek-speaking Mycenaeans take control of Crete and other southern Aegean islands, which had long been ruled by the Minoans, culturally advanced non-Greek speakers.

ca. 1200
Traditional date for the Trojan War, a Mycenaean raiding expedition later memorialized in Homer's epic poem, the *Iliad*.

ca. 1100–800
Greece's Dark Age, in which poverty and illiteracy are at first widespread and city-states begin to emerge.

ca. 800–500
The Greek Archaic Age, characterized by the return of prosperity and literacy, rapid population growth, and intensive colonization of the Mediterranean and Black Seas.

ca. 630
Birth of the Athenian lawgiver Solon, the first Greek political figure whose writings have survived.

594
The Athenians make Solon archon (administrator), charging him with the task of revising the city's social and political system.

561
Solon's kinsman, the tyrant Pisistratus, takes control of the state.

ca. 523
Birth of the distinguished Athenian politician-admiral Themistocles.

508
Building on Solon's reforms, an aristocrat named Cleisthenes transforms Athens's government into the world's first democracy.

ca. 500–323
Greece's Classic Age, in which Greek arts, architecture, literature, and democratic reforms reach their height.

495

Birth of the great Athenian democratic reformer and cultural patron Pericles.

493

Themistocles becomes archon and begins fortifying Athens's new port town, Piraeus.

490

The Athenians defeat a force of invading Persians at Marathon, northeast of Athens.

480

Themistocles engineers a major naval victory over the Persians at Salamis, southwest of Athens.

471

Themistocles is banished for ten years.

461

After the democratic reformer Ephialtes is assassinated, Pericles becomes the most influential leader in Athens.

457

Pericles finishes construction of the Long Walls, a fortified corridor leading from Piraeus to Athens's urban center; the Athenians and Spartans clash at Tanagra, near Thebes.

ca. 450

Birth of the infamous Greek traitor Alcibiades.

431

The disastrous Peloponnesian War, which will engulf and exhaust almost all the city-states, begins.

429

A deadly plague strikes Athens, killing a large number of residents, including Pericles.

415

At Alcibiades' urging, the Athenians send a large military expedition to Sicily in hopes of conquering the Greek city of Syracuse; when the ships arrive in Sicily, Alcibiades deserts his countrymen.

410

Alcibiades scores his biggest military success, defeating the Spartans at Cyzicus, south of the Black Sea; the renowned Theban general Epaminondas is born.

404

Athens surrenders, ending the great war.

ca. 382

Birth of Philip, the Macedonian king destined to conquer and briefly unite the Greeks.

371
Epaminondas defeats the Spartans at Leuctra, near Thebes, forever shattering the myth of Spartan invincibility.

360
Epaminondas dies in battle.

338
Philip and his teenage son, Alexander, defeat an allied Greek army at Chaeronea, in central Greece.

336
Philip is assassinated and Alexander, who will one day be called "the Great," ascends Macedonia's throne.

323
After invading Persia and creating the largest empire the world has yet seen, Alexander dies in the Persian capital of Babylon.

ca. 323–31
Greece's Hellenistic Age, in which Alexander's successors carve up his empire into several new kingdoms and frequently war among themselves, and Rome steadily gains control of the Greek world.

ca. 319
Birth of Pyrrhus, a prince of the small Greek kingdom of Epirus, who will become one of the leading military strongmen of the age.

280
Pyrrhus answers a call for help from Tarentum, a Greek city in southern Italy that has been threatened by Rome; Pyrrhus narrowly defeats the Romans at Heraclea, near Tarentum.

275
Pyrrhus, having been unable to make decisive headway against the Romans, abandons Italy, leaving the Italian Greeks to fend for themselves.

168
The Greek Macedonian kingdom comes under Roman domination.

31
Cleopatra VII, last of the Greek Hellenistic monarchs, is defeated by the Romans at Actium, in western Greece.

FOR FURTHER READING

Isaac Asimov, *The Greeks: A Great Adventure*. Boston: Houghton Mifflin, 1965. An excellent, entertaining overview of Greek history and culture.

David Bellingham, *An Introduction to Greek Mythology*. Secaucus, NJ: Chartwell Books, 1989. Explains the major Greek myths and legends and their importance to the ancient Greeks. Contains many beautiful photos and drawings.

C. M. Bowra, *Classical Greece*. New York: Time-Life Books, 1965. Despite the passage of more than thirty years, this volume, written by a renowned classical historian and adorned with numerous maps, drawings, and color photos, is only slightly dated and remains one of the best introductions to ancient Greece for general readers.

Peter Connolly, *The Greek Armies*. Morristown, NJ: Silver Burdett, 1979. A fine, detailed study of Greek armor, weapons, and battle tactics, filled with colorful, accurate illustrations by Connolly, the world's leading artistic interpreter of the ancient world. Highly recommended.

Denise Dersin, *Greece: Temples, Tombs, and Treasures*. Alexandria, VA: Time-Life Books, 1994. In a way a newer companion volume to Bowra's book (see above), this is also excellent and features a long, up-to-date, and beautifully illustrated chapter on Athens's golden age.

Rhoda A. Hendricks, trans., *Classical Gods and Heroes*. New York: Morrow Quill, 1974. A collection of easy-to-read translations of famous Greek myths and tales, as told by ancient Greek and Roman writers, including Homer, Hesiod, Pindar, Apollodorus, Ovid, and Virgil.

Author's Note: In the following volumes I provide much useful background information about Greek history and culture, including the Greek-Persian conflict; the rise and fall of the Athenian empire; the golden age of arts, literature, and architecture; the rise of Thebes and Macedonia; the consequences of Alexander's conquests; and sketches of the important Greek politicians, military leaders, writers, and artists.

Don Nardo, *Greek and Roman Theater*. San Diego: Lucent Books, 1995.

———, *The Battle of Marathon*. San Diego: Lucent Books, 1996.

———, *The Age of Pericles*. San Diego: Lucent Books, 1996.

———, *Life in Ancient Greece*. San Diego: Lucent Books, 1996.

———, *The Trial of Socrates*. San Diego: Lucent Books, 1997.

———, *Scientists of Ancient Greece*. San Diego: Lucent Books, 1998.

———, *The Parthenon*. San Diego: Lucent Books, 1999.

———, *Greek and Roman Sport*. San Diego: Lucent Books, 1999.

Susan Peach and Anne Millard, *The Greeks*. London: Usborne, 1990. A general overview of the history, culture, myths, and everyday life of ancient Greece, presented in a format suitable to young, basic readers (although the many fine, accurate color illustrations make the book appealing to anyone interested in ancient Greece).

Jonathon Rutland, *See Inside an Ancient Greek Town*. New York: Barnes and Noble, 1995. This colorful introduction to ancient Greek life is aimed at basic readers.

John Warry, *Warfare in the Classical World*. Norman: University of Oklahoma Press, 1980 and 1995. A beautifully mounted book filled with accurate and useful paintings, drawings, maps, and diagrams. The text is also first-rate, providing much detailed information about the weapons, clothing, strategies, battle tactics, and military leaders of the Greeks, Romans, and the peoples they fought.

Alcibiades

Ancient Sources

Most extensive ancient source:
Thucydides, *The Peloponnesian War,* published as *The Landmark Thucydides.* Trans. Richard Crawley, ed. Robert S. Strassler. New York: Simon and Schuster, 1996.

Also important:
Cornelius Nepos, *The Book of the Great Generals of Foreign Nations.* Trans. John C. Rolfe. Cambridge, MA: Harvard University Press, 1960.

Plutarch, *Life of Alcibiades,* in *The Rise and Fall of Athens: Nine Greek Lives by Plutarch.* Trans. Ian Scott-Kilvert. New York: Penguin Books, 1960. Plutarch also mentions Alcibiades in his portraits of Nicias and Lysander.

Xenophon, *Hellenica,* published as *A History of My Times.* Trans. Rex Warner. New York: Penguin Books, 1979.

Several brief descriptions of ancient paintings and statues of Alcibiades in:
Pausanias, *Guide to Greece.* 2 vols. Trans. Peter Levi. New York: Penguin Books, 1971.

Pliny the Elder, *Natural History,* excerpted in *Pliny the Elder: Natural History, A Selection.* Trans. John F. Healy. New York: Penguin Books, 1991.

Alcibiades appears as a character in:
Plato, *Symposium,* in *Symposium of Plato.* Trans. Tom Griffith. Berkeley and Los Angeles: University of California Press, 1985. The reader should be aware that Alcibiades' character in this Platonic dialogue is more fictional than real.

Modern Sources

Book-length study:
Walter M. Ellis, *Alcibiades.* New York: Routledge, 1989.

Less detailed but sufficient descriptions of Alcibiades' career in:
Victor Ehrenberg, *From Solon to Socrates.* London: Methuen, 1968.

Donald Kagan, *The Peace of Nicias and the Sicilian Expedition.* Ithaca: Cornell University Press, 1981; and *The Fall of the Athenian Empire.* Ithaca: Cornell University Press, 1987. These works are part of Kagan's masterly four-part series on the Peloponnesian conflict that has been rightly called one of the major achievements of modern historical scholarship.

Russell Meiggs, *The Athenian Empire*. Oxford: Clarendon Press, 1972.

Alexander

Ancient Sources

Most important ancient sources for Alexander and his conquests:

Arrian, *Anabasis Alexandri*, published as *The Campaigns of Alexander*. Trans. Aubrey de Sélincourt. New York: Penguin Books, 1971.

Diodorus Siculus, *Library of History*, Book 17. Trans. Charles L. Sherman and C. Bradford Welles. Cambridge, MA: Harvard University Press, 1963.

Plutarch, *Life of Alexander*, in *The Age of Alexander*. Trans. Ian Scott-Kilvert. New York: Penguin Books, 1973. Plutarch also provides information about Alexander in his lives of Demosthenes, Phocion, and Eumenes, as well as in his *Moralia* (especially the essay titled *On the Fortune or Virtue of Alexander*).

Quintus Curtius Rufus, *History of Alexander*. Trans. John Yardley. New York: Penguin Books, 1984.

Modern Sources

Given Alexander's towering reputation, the modern literature on him is huge.

Among the most detailed and reliable general studies are:

Robin Lane Fox, *Alexander the Great*. London: Allan Lane, 1973.

Peter Green, *Alexander of Macedon, 356–323 B.C.: A Historical Biography*. Berkeley and Los Angeles: University of California Press, 1991. Arguably the best recent general work about Alexander.

N. G. L. Hammond, *The Genius of Alexander the Great*. Chapel Hill: University of North Carolina Press, 1997.

John M. O'Brien, *Alexander the Great: The Invisible Enemy*. New York: Routledge, 1994. An entertaining and worthwhile read, with an excellent up-to-date bibliography.

W. W. Tarn, *Alexander the Great*. 2 vols. Cambridge: Cambridge University Press, 1979. A very readable but somewhat overly romantic treatment.

Ulrich Wilcken, *Alexander the Great*. Trans. G. C. Richards. New York: Dial Press, 1932. New edition, with notes and bibliography by E. N. Borza, 1967. Dated but still useful.

For analyses of Alexander's military prowess, army, and campaigns, see:

Donald W. Engels, *Alexander the Great and the Logistics of the Macedonian Army*. Berkeley and Los Angeles: University of California Press, 1978.

J. F. C. Fuller, *The Generalship of Alexander the Great*. New Brunswick, NJ: Rutgers University Press, 1960. The classic of its kind.

Nick Sekunda and John Warry, *Alexander the Great: His Armies and Campaigns, 334–323 B.C.* London: Osprey, 1998. A beautifully illustrated volume.

A shorter, less scholarly, and heavily illustrated overview:

Pierre Briant, *Alexander the Great: Man of Action, Man of Spirit*. New York: Harry N. Abrams, 1996.

Epaminondas

Ancient Sources

It is tragic that Plutarch's biography of Epaminondas did not survive, partly because so few other ancient sources cover the great Theban leader in any detail, and also because Epaminondas was Plutarch's favorite historical character (therefore the lost work likely covered Epaminondas and his career in detail and with loving care).

Most extensive primary source information in:

Cornelius Nepos, *The Book of the Great Generals of Foreign Nations*. Trans. John C. Rolfe. Cambridge, MA: Harvard University Press, 1960.

Diodorus Siculus, *Library of History*, (Book 15). 12 vols. Trans. Charles L. Sherman and C. Bradford Welles. Cambridge, MA: Harvard University Press, 1963.

Plutarch, *Life of Pelopidas* and *Life of Agesilaus*, in *The Age of Alexander: Nine Greek Lives by Plutarch*. Trans. Ian Scott-Kilvert. New York: Penguin, 1973; and various sections of *Moralia* (or *Moral Essays*), excerpted in *Plutarch: Essays*. Trans. Robin Waterfield. New York: Penguin Books, 1992.

Polybius, *The Histories*, in *Polybius: The Rise of the Roman Empire*. Trans. Ian Scott-Kilvert. New York: Penguin Books, 1979.

Xenophon, *Hellenica*, Book 7. Published as *A History of My Times*. Trans. Rex Warner. New York: Penguin Books, 1979.

Modern Sources

Discussions of Epaminondas and his military innovations in:

J. K. Anderson, *Military Theory and Practice in the Age of Xenophon*. Berkeley and Los Angeles: University of California Press, 1970.

R. J. Buck, *A History of Boeotia*. Edmonton: University of Alberta Press, 1979.

J. Buckler, *The Theban Hegemony, 371–362 B.C.* Cambridge, MA: Harvard University Press, 1980.

Some briefer but useful references in:

Frank E. Adcock, *The Greek and Macedonian Art of War*. Berkeley and Los Angeles: University of California Press, 1957.

Victor D. Hanson, *The Western Way to War: Infantry Battle in Classical Greece*. New York: Oxford University Press, 1989. An informative and riveting description of hoplite warfare. Highly recommended.

Pericles

Ancient Sources

Most important primary sources:

Aristotle, *Athenian Constitution*. Trans. H. Rackham. 1952. Reprint, Cambridge, MA: Harvard University Press, 1996; and *Politics*. Ed. and trans. Ernest Baker. New York: Oxford University Press, 1946.

Plutarch, *Life of Pericles*, in *The Rise and Fall of Athens*. Trans. Ian Scott-Kilvert. New York: Penguin Books, 1960.

Thucydides, *The Peloponnesian War*, published as *The Landmark Thucydides: A Comprehensive Guide to the Peloponnesian War*. Trans. Richard Crawley, ed. Robert B. Strassler. New York: Simon and Schuster, 1996; another excellent translation is by Rex Warner (New York: Penguin Books, 1972).

Xenophon, *Hellenica*, published as *A History of My Times*. Trans. Rex Warner. New York: Penguin Books, 1979.

Pericles and his mistress, Aspasia, lampooned by the Athenian comic playwright Aristophanes in:

Acharnians, trans. B. B. Rogers, in Moses Hadas, ed., *The Complete Plays of Aristophanes*. New York: Bantam Books, 1962.

Modern Sources

Among the fullest and best-documented general studies of Pericles' career and the age bearing his name are:

C. M. Bowra, *Periclean Athens*. New York: Dial Press, 1971.

Donald Kagan, *Pericles of Athens and the Birth of Democracy*. New York: Free Press, 1991.

Charles A. Robinson, *Athens in the Age of Pericles*. Norman: University of Oklahoma Press, 1959.

Useful shorter treatments:

"The Great Fifty Years, I, II, and III," in Andrew R. Burn, *The Penguin History of Greece*. New York: Penguin Books, 1985, pp. 193–257.

Michael Grant, *The Classical Greeks*. New York: Scribner's, 1989.

Pericles' contributions to Athenian democracy:

J. K. Davies, *Democracy and Classical Greece*. Cambridge, MA: Harvard University Press, 1993.

W. G. Forrest, *The Emergence of Greek Democracy*. New York: World University Library, 1966.

Later political activities, leading into the Peloponnesian War:
Donald Kagan, *The Outbreak of the Peloponnesian War*. Ithaca, NY: Cornell University Press, 1969.

A thorough and entertaining sketch of Aspasia and her niche in Periclean Athens in:
Robert B. Kebric, *Greek People*. Mountain View, CA: Mayfield Publishing, 1997, chapter 6.

Philip

Ancient Sources

Main ancient source:
Diodorus Siculus, *Library of History*, (Book 16). 12 vols. Trans. Charles L. Sherman and C. Bradford Welles. Cambridge, MA: Harvard University Press, 1963. It is both fortunate and unfortunate that most of what we know about Philip and his career comes from Diodorus's history. It is fortunate because Diodorus preserved a good deal of information from other histories now either lost or extant only in fragments, perhaps most notably the *Philippica* (*History of Philip*) of the fourth-century B.C. Greek historian Theopompus. It is unfortunate because Diodorus's writing is uninspired, uncritical, and often unreliable; modern scholars must be cautious when consulting his material.

Supplementary ancient sources include:
Arrian, *Anabasis Alexandri*, published as *The Campaigns of Alexander*. Trans. Aubrey de Sélincourt. New York: Penguin Books, 1971.
Demosthenes, speeches, in *Olynthiacs, Philippics, Minor Speeches*. Trans. J. H. Vince. Cambridge, MA: Harvard University Press, 1962.
Isocrates, speeches, in *Isocrates*. Trans. George Norlin. Cambridge MA: Harvard University Press, 1928.
Plutarch, *Life of Demosthenes*, in *The Age of Alexander: Nine Greek Lives by Plutarch*. Trans. Ian Scott-Kilvert. New York: Penguin Books, 1973; and various sections of *Moralia* (or *Moral Essays*), excerpted in *Plutarch: Essays*. Trans. Robin Waterfield. New York: Penguin Books, 1992.

Modern Sources

First major modern study:
David Hogarth, *Philip and Alexander of Macedon*. 1897. Reprint, Freeport, NY: Books for the Libraries Press, 1971. Though dated, this remains useful for scholars and Macedonia buffs. The last thirty years have witnessed an upsurge in scholarly interest in Philip, one that largely agrees with Professor Hogarth's thesis that Alexander owed many of his military ideas and much of his success to Philip.

Among the best of the more recent studies:

Eugene Borza, *In the Shadow of Olympus: The Emergence of Macedon*. Princeton, NJ: Princeton University Press, 1990. Nicely chronicles Philip's early deeds and is also invaluable for its detailed overview of Philip's Macedonian predecessors.

George Cawkwell, *Philip of Macedon*. Boston: Faber and Faber, 1978.

J. R. Ellis, *Philip II and Macedonian Imperialism*. Princeton, NJ: Princeton University Press, 1976. Contains excellent discussions of Philip's possible motives and goals.

N. G. L. Hammond, *Philip of Macedon*. Baltimore: Johns Hopkins University Press, 1994.

Miltiades B. Hatzopoulos and Louisa D. Loukopoulos, *Philip of Macedon*. Athens: Ekdotike Athenon, 1980. A collection of essays by noted scholars.

Pyrrhus

Ancient Sources

Unfortunately, the period from 281 to 221 B.C., encompassing the heart, so to speak, of the Hellenistic Age, including most of Pyrrhus's famous exploits, is one of the most poorly documented in all of ancient history. Luckily, some information about the famous Hellenistic king of Epirus survives in the works of writers who had access to now lost histories of that period.

Most notable ancient accounts:

Plutarch, *Life of Pyrrhus* and *Life of Demetrius*, in *The Age of Alexander*. Trans. Ian Scott-Kilvert. New York: Penguin Books, 1973.

Polybius *The Histories*, in *Polybius: The Rise of the Roman Empire*. Trans. Ian Scott-Kilvert. New York: Penguin Books, 1979.

Briefer mentions of Pyrrhus in:

Appian, *Roman History*. 4 vols. Trans. Horace White. Cambridge, MA: Harvard University Press, 1964.

Livy, *History of Rome from Its Founding*, excerpted in *Livy: Rome and Italy*. Trans. Betty Radice. New York: Penguin Books, 1982; and *Livy: The War with Hannibal*. Trans. Aubrey de Sélincourt. New York: Penguin Books, 1972.

Modern Sources

Book-length study:

Petros Garouphalias, *Pyrrhus*. London: Stacey International, 1979. Out of print and difficult to find.

General overviews of Pyrrhus's exploits in:

Peter Green, *Alexander to Actium: The Historical Evolution of the Hellenistic Age*. Berkeley and Los Angeles: University of California

Press, 1990. By far the most complete and well-documented available study of the Hellenistic Age.

Erich Gruen, *The Hellenistic World and the Coming of Rome*. Berkeley and Los Angeles: University of California Press, 1984.

N. G. L. Hammond, *Epirus*. Oxford: Oxford University Press, 1967.

Less extensive treatments of Pyrrhus appear in:

T. J. Cornell, *The Beginnings of Rome*. New York: Routledge, 1995.

Michael Grant, *History of Rome*. New York: Scribner's, 1978; and *From Alexander to Cleopatra: The Hellenistic Age*. New York: Scribner's, 1982.

Solon

Ancient Sources

The most extensive ancient source:

Plutarch, *Life of Solon*, in *The Rise and Fall of Athens: Nine Greek Lives by Plutarch*. Trans. Ian Scott-Kilvert. New York: Penguin, 1960.

Other important ancient sources:

Aristotle, *The Athenian Constitution*, in *The Athenian Constitution, Eudemian Ethics, Virtues and Vices*. Trans. H. Rackham. 1952. Reprint, Cambridge, MA: Harvard University Press, 1996.

Herodotus, *The Histories*. Trans. Aubrey de Sélincourt. New York: Penguin Books, 1972.

Plato, *Timaeus*, in *The Dialogues of Plato*. Trans. Benjamin Jowett. Great Books of the Western World. Chicago: Encyclopaedia Britannica, 1952.

For Solon's own poems, see:

Kenneth J. Atchity, ed., *The Classical Greek Reader*. New York: Oxford University Press, 1996. Contains selected excerpts from the poems.

Kathleen Freeman, *The Work and Life of Solon, with a Translation of His Poems*. Cardiff: University of Wales Press, 1926. Reprint, New York: Arno, 1976. Contains complete surviving poems.

Modern Sources

Book-length studies:

Kathleen Freeman, *The Work and Life of Solon, with a Translation of His Poems*. Cardiff: University of Wales Press, 1926. Reprint, New York: Arno, 1976.

Ivan F. Linforth, *Solon the Athenian*. 1919. Reprint, Berkeley and Los Angeles: University of California Press, 1971.

William J. Woodhouse, *Solon the Liberator*. London: Oxford University Press, 1938. Reprint, New York: Octagon Books, 1965.

Shorter but informative sketches in:
Victor Ehrenberg, *From Solon to Socrates*. London: Methuen, 1968.
Michael Grant, *The Rise of the Greeks*. New York: Macmillan, 1987.

Themistocles

Ancient Sources

Most detailed and reliable ancient accounts:
Herodotus, *The Histories*. Trans. Aubrey de Sélincourt. New York:
Penguin Books, 1972.
Plutarch, *Life of Themistocles,* in *The Rise and Fall of Athens: Nine
Greek Lives by Plutarch*. Trans. Ian Scott-Kilvert. New York:
Penguin, 1960. Plutarch also mentions Themistocles in his lives
of Aristides and Cimon (also in *The Rise and Fall of Athens*).
Thucydides, *The Peloponnesian War*, published as *The Landmark
Thucydides: A Comprehensive Guide to the Peloponnesian War*.
Trans. Richard Crawley, ed. Robert B. Strassler. New York: Si-
mon and Schuster, 1996; another excellent translation is by Rex
Warner (New York: Penguin Books, 1972).

Less reliable but still historically important:
Aeschylus, *The Persians,* in *Aeschylus: Prometheus Bound, The Sup-
pliants, Seven Against Thebes, The Persians*. Trans. Philip Vella-
cott. Baltimore: Penguin Books, 1961.
Cornelius Nepos, *The Book of the Great Generals of Foreign Na-
tions*. Trans. John C. Rolfe. Cambridge, MA: Harvard University
Press, 1960.
Diodorus Siculus, *Library of History* (or *Universal History*). 12 vols.
Trans. Charles L. Sherman and C. Bradford Welles. Cambridge,
MA: Harvard University Press, 1963.

Modern Sources

R. J. Leonardon, *The Saga of Themistocles*. London: Thames and
Hudson, 1978.
A. J. Podlecki, *The Life of Themistocles*. Montreal: McGill-Queen's
University Press, 1975. Contains an excellent in-depth discussion
of all the ancient sources.

A useful short biography in:
Michael Grant, *The Classical Greeks*. New York: Scribner's, 1989.

Studies of the Greek and Persian wars, in which Themistocles' char-
acter looms large:
Andrew R. Burn, *Persia and the Greeks: The Defense of the West,* c.
546–478 B.C. London: Edward Arnold, 1962.
Peter Green, *The Greco-Persian Wars*. Berkeley and Los Angeles:
University of California Press, 1996.
John Lazenby, *The Defense of Greece*. Bloomington, IL: David
Brown, 1993.

Additional Sources Consulted

Charles D. Adams, *Demosthenes and His Influence*. New York: Cooper Square Publishers, 1963.

Lesly Adkins and Roy A. Adkins, *Handbook to Life in Ancient Greece*. New York: Facts On File, 1997.

C. M. Bowra, *The Greek Experience*. New York: New American Library, 1957.

——, *Classical Greece*. New York: Time-Life Books, 1965.

Walter Burkert, *Greek Religion, Archaic and Classical*. Oxford: Basil Blackwell, 1985.

J. B. Bury, *A History of Greece to the Death of Alexander*. Rev. Russell Meiggs. London: Macmillan, 1975.

L. Sprague de Camp, *The Ancient Engineers*. New York: Ballantine Books, 1963.

Peter Connolly, *Greece and Rome at War*. London: Greenhill Books, 1998.

John A. Crow, *Greece: The Magic Spring*. New York: Harper and Row, 1970.

M. I. Finley, *The Ancient Greeks: An Introduction to Their Life and Thought*. New York: Viking Press, 1964.

Michael Grant, *Myths of the Greeks and Romans*. New York: Penguin Books, 1962.

——, *Greek and Roman Historians: Information and Misinformation*. London: Routledge, 1995.

——, *A Guide to the Ancient World*. New York: Barnes and Noble, 1996.

Peter Green, *The Parthenon*. New York: Newsweek Book Division, 1973.

G. T. Griffith, *Mercenaries of the Hellenistic World*. New York: AMS, 1977.

Sir John Hackett, ed., *Warfare in the Ancient World*. New York: Facts On File, 1989.

Victor D. Hanson, *The Other Greeks: The Family Farm and the Agrarian Roots of Western Civilization*. New York: Simon and Schuster, 1995.

Werner Jaeger, *Demosthenes*. Berkeley: University of California Press, 1938.

Bernard Knox, ed., *The Norton Book of Classical Literature*. New York: W. W. Norton, 1993.

Peter Levi, *Atlas of the Greek World*. New York: Facts On File, 1984.

Naphtali Lewis, *Life in Egypt Under Roman Rule*. Oxford: Clarendon Press, 1983.

Thomas R. Martin, *Ancient Greece: From Prehistoric to Hellenistic Times*. New Haven, CT: Yale University Press, 1996.

Evi Melas, *Temples and Sanctuaries of Ancient Greece*. London: Thames and Hudson, 1973.

John Miliadis, *The Acropolis*. Athens: M. Pechlivanidis, n.d.

G. M. A. Richter, *Portraits of the Greeks*. Rev. R. R. R. Smith. Ithaca: Cornell University Press, 1984.

Aubrey de Sélincourt, *The World of Herodotus*. San Francisco: North Point Press, 1982.

Nigel Spivey, *Greek Art*. London: Phaidon, 1997.

Chester G. Starr, *A History of the Ancient World*. New York: Oxford University Press, 1991.

INDEX

Achilles, 14, 83, 92
acropolis, Greek, 15, 19, 27
Acropolis complex, 51–52
Actium, battle of, 24
Adcock, Frank E., 65, 87
Aeacides, 92
Aegean, 14, 17
Aegospotami, battle of, 64
Aeschylus, 43
Agariste, 48
Agelaus of Aetolia, 24
Age of Heroes, 14, 16
    see also Bronze Age
Agesilaus, 67
Alcibiades
    character of, 57
    death of, 64
    expedition of, to Sicily, 60–62
    foreign policy of, 59–60
    is exiled, 64
    as traitor, 61–62
    victory of, at Cyzicus, 63
    youth of, 58–59
Alexander II. See Alexander the Great
Alexander the Great, 75
    battle in India by, 90
    birth of, 22, 78, 82
    conquest of Persian Empire by,
        22–23, 88–89
    death of, 90
    early conquests of, 84–85
    education of, by Aristotle, 84
    jealousy of Philip's successes and,
        83–84
    as king of Macedonia, 85–86
    military and political tactics of,
        86–87
    philosophy of, 83
Alexandria, Egypt, 89
Amphipolis, 78
Amyntas III, 74, 75
Anaxagoras, 55
Antigone, 93
Antigonus, 92, 93
Archaic Age, 16–18
Archippe, 36
archons (public administrators), 27
Areopagus, Council of, 27–28, 37, 49
Argos, 96

Aristotle
    on the Areopagus, 27, 49
    on debt bondage, 30
    as tutor of Alexander the Great, 84
Arrian
    on Alexander the Great, 90
    on battle at Granicus River, 88–89
Artaxerxes, 45
Artemis, 82
Asia Minor, 13, 23, 40, 48, 63
Aspasia, 55
Assembly (*Ecclesia*), Athenian, 27,
    32, 60, 62
Athena, 19, 51
Athens
    Acropolis complex in, 51–52
    Aegospotami and, 64
    during Dark Age, 15
    Delian League and, 53
    dispute with Megara, 26
    Egyptian expedition by, 53
    golden age of, 46
    hostile relations between Thebes
        and, 71
    Long Walls of, 50, 54
    new democracy of, 18, 36–37
    Parthenon in, 19, 51–52
    in Peloponnesian War
        defeat of, 21, 56, 64
        Peace of Nicias and, 60
    in Persian wars
        at Marathon, 18, 38
        at Salamis, 19, 35, 40–43
    plague in, 56
    rivalry between Sparta and, 20–21,
        54
    social and political reforms in,
        27–32
    Syracuse campaign of, 60–62
    Tanagra and, 54
        see also Alcibiades; Pericles;
        Solon; Themistocles
Atlantis, 33
Attica, 27, 42
Ausculum, Italy, 95

Babylon, 89, 90
Black Sea, 17, 63
boeotarch (Theban general), 67

124

PICTURE CREDITS

ABOUT THE AUTHOR

Classical historian and award-winning writer Don Nardo has published more than thirty books about the ancient Greek and Roman world. These include general histories, such as *The Roman Empire, The Persian Empire*, and *The Age of Pericles;* cultural studies such as *Life in Ancient Greece, Greek and Roman Theater, The Parthenon, Life of a Roman Slave*, and *Scientists of Ancient Greece;* biographies of Julius Caesar and Cleopatra; and literary companions to the works of Homer and Sophocles. Mr. Nardo also writes screenplays and teleplays and composes music. He lives with his lovely wife, Christine, and dog, Bud, on Cape Cod, Massachusetts.